Dl

 St. Louis Community College

Forest Park
Florissant Valley
Meramec

Instructional Resources
St. Louis, Missouri

Springer Series on Social Work

Albert R. Roberts, Ph.D., Series Editor

Graduate School of Social Work, Rutgers,
The State University of New Jersey

Advisory Board: Gloria Bonilla-Santiago, Ph.D., Barbara Berkman, Ph.D., Elaine P. Congress, D.S.W., Sheldon R. Gelman, Ph.D., Gilbert J. Greene, Ph.D., Jesse Harris, D.S.W., C. Aaron McNeece, D.S.W.

Namkee G. Choi, MSW, Ph.D, is an associate professor at the School of Social Work, SUNY at Buffalo, where she teaches social problems, social policy, aging policy, and research methods.

Lidia J. Snyder, MSW, is a social worker at Berkshire Farm Center and Services for Youth in Buffalo, New York.

HOMELESS FAMILIES WITH CHILDREN

A Subjective Experience of Homelessness

Namkee G. Choi, MSW, PhD
Lidia J. Snyder, MSW

SPRINGER PUBLISHING COMPANY
NEW YORK

Springer Publishing Company, Inc.
536 Broadway
New York, NY 10012-3955

Acquisitions Editor: Bill Tucker
Production Editor: Barbara Beard Trocco
Cover design by: James Scotto-Lavino
Cover photo: Alice Marino

99 00 01 02 03 / 5 4 3 2 1

Choi, Namkes G., 1955–
    Homeless families with children : a subjective experience of homelessness / Namkee G. Choi and Lidia J. Snyder.
        p.   cm. — (Springer series on social work)
    Includes bibliographical references and index.
    ISBN 0-8261-1285-4
    1. Homeless families—United States.   2. Homeless children—United States.   3. Homeless persons—Services for—United States.
    4. Homelessness. 5. Family social work—United States.
    I. Snyder, Lidia J.   II. Title.   III. Series.
HV4505.C46   1999
362.5'85'0973—dc21   99–15738
                                                                          CIP

Printed in the United States of America

Contents

Preface

This book was written with two purposes in mind. First, we attempt to inform readers of the direct association between poverty and deepening problems of urban decline and increasing homelessness among families in the 1980s and the 1990s. Second, we intend to give homeless families an opportunity to be heard regarding their own perception of the causes, effects, and possible solutions of their homelessness.

Although homelessness has become one of the most frequently studied social problems in recent decades, its relationship to the deterioration of our inner cities and the spatial isolation of the poor has not been examined. As a result, policies and programs that were designed to deal with the problems of homelessness and homeless families have been inadequate. By listening to the stories of 80 homeless parents in this book, we hope the readers fully understand the connection among economic depression, dilapidated neighborhood conditions, the concentration of joblessness and poverty, and a simultaneous concentration of illegal substance abuse, crime, violence, family disruption, and homelessness in poor urban areas.

We present these parents' stories in their own voices. Eloquently they relate their humiliation, frustration, and indignation and their children's suffering in dealing with the extremely harsh reality of being homeless. Secure and affordable housing is the most important basic human need, without which parents and children cannot sustain physical and emotional well-being. Becoming homeless thus posed the most serious threat to these families' survival. The families were fully aware of this threat. They were also aware that they lacked resources to deal with the crisis. Hence, in the last chapter, we recommend policies and programs that would not only assist these families to secure affordable permanent housing but also prevent homelessness. We credit the homeless families for their insight and suggestions for the content of the last chapter.

We hope that the book makes a modest contribution to understanding the causes and effects of homelessness among poor families. We believe that this book may prove to serve as a critically important resource for social work students and faculty who study social problems of poverty, homelessness, and displaced populations. Social work practitioners who work with poor families who are homeless or at risk of becoming homeless will similarly find this book informative and helpful in developing further insight to the families' problems in the context. Social policy and lawmakers, as well as social work practitioners, will also find the program and policy recommendations timely and practical.

We are indebted to many colleagues and friends for their encouragement and warm assistance. Special thanks are extended to the members and staff of the Baldy Center for Law and Social Policy, the State University of New York (SUNY) at Buffalo, which provided financial support for the study. Grateful acknowledgments are made to David Engel, Laura Mangan, Murray Levine, Frank Munger, Howard Doueck, Anne Gaulin, and Rebecca Roblee. We would also like to acknowledge the financial support of Jerome D. and Marilyn Z. Shine. We thank Dean Lawrence Shulman and the faculty and staff of the School of Social Work, SUNY at Buffalo, for their constant encouragement. We thank Kim Wurapa, Mary Houghteling, and Christine Jaimes for their assistance with the interviews. We thank Loretta Sauer and Betsy Tuttlebee for their assistance. We were much moved by their compassion and professionalism. We were also fortunate to receive insightful and most valuable comments from Professors Albert Roberts of the State University at Rutgers, John Wodarski of SUNY at Buffalo, Pat Brownell of Fordham University, and C. Aaron McNeece of Florida State University. Special thanks are extended to Dr. Albert Roberts for his constant support and advocacy for the publication of the book.

We express our most enduring gratitude to the 80 homeless parents who opened their hearts to us. Without their willingness to participate in the study, this book would not have been possible. We dedicate this book to them. This book is theirs, their story.

NAMKEE G. CHOI
LIDIA J. SNYDER
APRIL 1, 1999

1

Understanding Homelessness Among Families: Causes, Effects, Policies, and Programs

Over the past two decades, those who study poverty and advocate for the poor have come to recognize the plight of the increasing numbers of homeless as one of the most serious social problems in the United States. Hundreds of articles and books have been published on the subject of homelessness and homeless people, and many serious accounts of their plight, as well as superficial descriptions of their mental illness or substance abuse problems, have appeared in major newspapers. In 1987 the federal government passed a major homeless assistance act. Thousands of temporary shelters have sprouted up in cities where the homeless have become as common as high-rise buildings. Although considerable effort has been invested in research, policy, and programs aimed at ameliorating the problem of homelessness, its magnitude has not been abated. Not only does the number of homeless people appear to be increasing, but an increasing share of them are families with young children.

1

The number of homeless people is a matter in dispute between govern- ments and advocates for the homeless (Kondratas, 1991; Mihaly, 1991; National Coalition for the Homeless [NCH], 1998a). One method of count- ing homeless people is to identify those who have been homeless for a lifetime or during a designated period. Two national telephone surveys conducted in 1991 and 1994, using this period-prevalence method, iden- tified, naturally, a much higher number of people who have been home- less previously than those who are currently homeless. For example, the 1994 survey found that, nationwide, 12 million adults had been literally homeless—that is, on the streets or in shelters—at some point in their lives and 6.6 million had been literally homeless or had lived doubled up between 1989 and 1994 (Link, Phelan, Bresnahan, Stueve, Moore, & Susser, 1995; NCH, 1998a).

But the most frequently cited number has been 500,000 to 600,000, estimated by two Urban Institute researchers by counting homeless people found in shelters, eating at soup kitchens, or congregating on the street during 1 week in 1988 (Burt & Cohen, 1989). That number and a projected 5% annual rate of increase yielded a 1996 estimate of 760,000 people homeless on any given night and 1.2 million to 2 million people who experience homelessness during 1 year (NCH, 1998a). Be- cause most homeless people, especially families with children, experi- ence only a brief period of literal homelessness, this point-in-time method of counting them may produce an overestimate of chronically homeless people. On the other hand, because not all homeless people show up in shelters or soup kitchens, congregate in the street, or identify themselves as homeless because they are afraid of being stigmatized, the same method of enumeration may produce an underestimate of the number of people who are homeless.

Most public and private sources agree that, on any given night, the number of homeless people is at least in the hundreds of thousands, without even counting those who live doubled up with relatives or friends. Moreover, all data indicate that poor families, headed by mostly minority, young, single mothers with children occupy an increasing share of the rank and file of the homeless (Rossi, 1994). A report by the U.S. Conference of Mayors estimated that, at the beginning of the 1990s, approximately one third of the homeless consisted of such fami- lies (U.S. Conference of Mayors, 1990). It was estimated that between one third and one half of those in homeless families were children (Mihaly, 1991). In its 1996 survey of 29 American cities, however, the U.S. Conference of Mayors found that families composed 38% of the homeless population; 45% were single men, and 14% were single women (Waxman & Hinderliter, 1996). The percentage of the homeless who were families with children was likely to be higher in rural areas, because research has found that such families make up the largest groups of homeless in rural areas (NCH, 1998a; Vissing, 1996). Most studies of the homeless also indicate that the number of both homeless and extremely poor families with children who are precariously housed and thus at risk of homelessness is also increasing.

  The cost of human suffering due to homelessness is manifested in the tens of thousands of poor families with children who sleep in temporary shelters or live doubled up with equally poor relatives or friends. Insecurity, instability, and uncertainty about the next meal and bed undoubtedly cause enormous stress and anguish and overwhelm adults and children alike. Despite parents' struggles to keep families together, shelter policies and overcrowded relatives' or friends' homes may force family members to be separated. Homeless children exhibit a host of health, developmental, and psychological problems, which interfere with their proper development and academic performance (Bassuk & Rosenberg, 1990; Bassuk & Weinreb, 1994; Rafferty, 1995). Homeless and near-homeless families who move from one dangerous neighborhood to another in deteriorating central cities are also susceptible to crime and violence on the city streets.

Previous research on homelessness, especially in mental health disciplines, has focused on personal deficits and pathologies, resulting in the medicalization of this devastating social problem and contributing to the depoliticizing of the problem (Snow, Anderson, & Koegel, 1994). Recently, however, as social scientists have become increasingly involved with the problems of homeless families, their economic predicament has been highlighted and the need for macro intervention has been emphasized. Most studies attribute homelessness among families with children to poverty and an insufficient supply of low-income affordable housing, not to personal pathology of family members. Unlike homeless individuals, a majority of homeless parents do not have the mental illness and/or substance abuse problems that often precipitate homelessness among singles. Homeless parents are more similar to poor domiciled parents than to homeless individuals.

The repeatedly substantiated connection between poverty and the shortage of low-income housing and homelessness among families has led those who study and analyze homelessness to prescribe employment, income maintenance, and low-income housing policies as effective intervention strategies. Nevertheless, the federal government has not been engaged in a systematic effort to solve the homeless problem, but has treated it as a temporary situation that deserves no more than emergency relief in the form of temporary shelters and other temporary

assistance. In the absence of systematic, structural government interventions to improve the economic status of the poor, through urban
revitalization, employment, and safety net programs, and to create
enough permanent housing for the homeless and near-homeless, the
number of homeless has been increasing and their plight continues.

In this chapter, we review existing research on homelessness among
families with children, focusing on its causes and effects on parents
and children, then we discuss the status of policies and programs that
have been designed to deal with it.

CAUSES OF HOMELESSNESS AMONG FAMILIES

Prior to the mid-1970s, a majority of the homeless were older single
males with substance (mostly alcohol) abuse and physical or mental
health problems who lived in urban skid row neighborhoods and were
rarely seen by the general public (Rossi, 1994). Most of those homeless
men were not literally shelterless but lived in single room occupancy
(SRO) hotels or found beds in other cheap accommodations (Rosenthal,
1994; Rossi, 1994). The current population of homeless single adults,
like their earlier counterparts, have much higher rates of mental illness,
substance abuse (alcohol as well as other drugs), and/or jail or prison
history than the domiciled population (McChesney, 1995). These disabilities may have been primary, and at least precipitating, factors causing
these individuals' homelessness, as was the case of their counterparts
in the 1950s and 1960s. Nevertheless, since the mid-1970s, the increase
in the number of homeless persons, both men and women, who are
literally shelterless and become increasingly visible in our city streets
indicates that factors other than the individuals' disabilities or personal
characteristics have also been at play. Previous studies have consistently shown that one of the most significant external factors was the
rapid disappearance of SROs due to urban renewal or redevelopment.

Homeless parents—an absolute majority of whom are single mothers—are also more likely than domiciled poor mothers to have abused
drugs. Thus, the mothers' drug abuse may have made poor families
more vulnerable to homelessness (Baum & Burnes, 1993; Jencks, 1994;
Weitzman, Knickman, & Shinn, 1992). In general, however, substance
abuse problems among homeless parents are much less prevalent than
among homeless individuals. Compared to their domiciled counterparts, the mostly single, minority women who head homeless families
also have higher incidences of psychiatric hospitalizations prior to having become homeless, but the rates were mostly in the single digits

(Shinn & Weitzman, 1996). Rates of psychiatric disorders tend to be higher among homeless parents than among poor housed parents. Some types of chronic psychiatric disorders, such as schizophrenia, antedate homelessness. Previous studies, however, present quite consistent evidence that depression in particular is more likely to follow than to precede homelessness, due to the severe stress that accompanies homelessness (Blau, 1992; McChesney, 1993).

Among families with children, domestic violence, rather than mental illness and/or substance abuse, has been identified as a significant cause of homelessness. Recent local estimates found that 25% to 35% of homeless women and children fled domestic abuse (NCH, 1998a). Previous studies also found that homeless mothers were more likely to have been battered as adults than were housed mothers (Bassuk, Browne, & Buckner, 1996; Bassuk & Rosenberg, 1988; Salomon, Bassuk, & Brooks, 1996). But again, Bassuk et al. (1996), in their multivariate modeling of housing status, did not find violence and its aftermath, such as depression and posttraumatic stress disorder (PTSD), to be significant factors distinguishing between poor housed mothers and homeless mothers. However, economic factors were the most salient in predicting the onset of homelessness.

Sociodemographic characteristics, among both the New York City sample and the Worcester County, Massachusetts, sample, show that homeless mothers tend to be younger and significantly more likely to be pregnant or to have a new baby than housed poor mothers (Brooks & Buckner, 1996; daCosta Nunez, 1994; Weitzman, 1989). A comparison between homeless families and a representative sample of low-income-family households in St. Louis city and county also found that the heads of homeless families are significantly younger and more likely to be never-married women of color. Housed and homeless families are not significantly different in number of children or in the educational level of the household head, but housed families are larger and have higher incomes, suggesting the presence of a second adult earner (Johnson, McChesney, Rocha, & Butterfield, 1995). Some studies also show that homeless mothers have less social support than do housed mothers (Bassuk & Rosenberg, 1988; McChesney, 1992), whereas others indicate that homeless families have more informal social support and rely on relatives and friends before becoming homeless but eventually wear out their welcome (Shinn, Knickman, & Weitzman, 1991; Wood, Valdez, Hayashi, & Shen, 1990). Social networks are often based on reciprocity, and homeless people have little to exchange and thus become isolated soon enough (Rosenthal, 1994).

Mental health and substance abuse problems, domestic violence as well as childhood victimization, the weight of parenting responsibilities at a young age, and the lack of social support for poor parents may certainly be factors precipitating many families' homelessness. Without the predisposing economic and housing conditions that make these families vulnerable, however, these problems alone would not necessarily precipitate them into homelessness. For example, the majority of women and their children leaving an abusive relationship do not become homeless. Only poor women who have nowhere to go or who are unable to afford an independent living arrangement in an expensive, competitive housing market become homeless.

Most researchers agree that family homelessness in the 1980s and the 1990s is primarily attributable to the increased number of the poor, especially poor single-female-headed families, and to the lack of affordable low-income housing units rather than to individual/behavioral deficits (Blau, 1992; DeAngelis, 1994; Johnson & Kreuger, 1989; Koegel, Burnam, & Baumohl, 1996; Leonard, Dolbeare, & Lazere, 1989; McChesney, 1990, 1993; Rosenthal, 1994; Rossi, 1989; Shinn & Gillespie, 1994; Shinn & Weitzman, 1996; Timmer, Eitzen, & Tally, 1994). These two factors—an increase in the number of the poor, especially poor minority single-female-headed families, and the declining stock of affordable low-income housing units—are the results of deindustrialization, a declining economic base and the deepening of racial segregation in many cities, an inadequate safety net, and inadequate low-income housing policies. Unless these structural barriers to improved living and housing conditions are dealt with, the plight of the homeless may not be alleviated.

Poverty, Lack of Affordable Low-Income Housing, and Rent Burdens

Between 1975 and 1993 the poverty rate increased from 12.3% of the population, or 25.9 million persons, to 15.1% of the population, or 39.3 million persons. The highest poverty rate was found among black and Hispanic single-female householders with children younger than age 18; in 1993, 57.7% of these black families and 60.5% of these Hispanic families were poor. Among white single-female-headed families, 39.6% were poor. (The number of poor single-female-headed households with children increased across race/ethnicity lines between 1975 and 1993. More than an 80% increase, from less than 1 million in 1975 to 1.8 million in 1993, was recorded for blacks; more than a 60% increase, from 1.3 million in 1975 to 2.1 million in 1993, was recorded for whites; and a 145% increase, from 288,000 in 1979 to 706,000 in 1993, was recorded for Hispanics.) Of the 39.3 million poor persons in 1993, children living with female householders accounted for 9.1 million, as compared to 5.6 million in 1975 (U.S. Bureau of the Census, 1995). In 1996, a year when the economy was strong and the poverty rate declined to 13.7%, or 36.5 million persons, the poverty rates among black and Hispanic single-female householders with children younger than age 18 did not decline but increased to 58.2% and 67.4%, respectively (U.S. Bureau of the Census, 1997).

The problem is not only the increased number of poor single mothers with children but also the erosion of incomes and worsening poverty among this group over the years. For example, the average incomes of the poorest 20% of single mothers with children were at 33% of the poverty level in 1973 and 1979, but they were at 26% and 25% in 1983 and 1989, respectively. The average poor female-headed family with children was surviving at only about half the poverty level in 1991 (Shinn & Gillespie, 1994). In 1996 about one third of the poor minority female-headed families with children under age 18 were living on incomes 50% below the poverty line (U.S. Bureau of the Census, 1997). These millions of poor female-headed families with children, together with increasing numbers of other poor families and individuals, are evidence that even the benefits of the robust economy in the mid- to late-1980s and again in the mid-1990s did not trickle down to those in the bottom economic strata.

For many of the poor, finding decent and affordable housing is an elusive goal that they cannot achieve. Poor homeowners are likely to have a hard time paying their mortgage. However, through economic booms and busts, poor renters are likely to have an even tougher time trying to bear increasing rent burdens. That is, while the incomes of these low-income renter households remained stagnant or dwindled, gross rents increased continuously over the past two decades. According to the State of the Nation's Housing report by the Joint Center for Housing Studies of Harvard University (1995), the median income of renter households, from 1970 to 1994, fell by 16%, to $15,814 annually, while gross rents increased more than 11%, to $403 monthly. Moreover, the largest rent increases were for units at the low end of the market. As a result, in 1990 some 43% (5.4 million) of all low-income renters (with incomes of $10,000 or less) paid more than half of their income for rent. A recent study by the National Low Income Housing Coalition (NLIHC, 1998) found that in 1997, a family of three in any major cities in any state in the country needed income well above the poverty line (167% of the poverty line in the median state) to afford the fair market rent for a two-bedroom rental unit ($558 in the median state) at 30% of their income.

Much of the rent hike is due to housing programs' having been cut back since the 1980s, squeezing subsidized and low-cost (monthly rent of $300 or less) unsubsidized housing units, despite increasing numbers of poor renters. That is, the increase in the number of poor households means the increase in the number of poor renters. Between 1985 and 1995 the number of very-low-income (with incomes less than 50% of area median) renter households jumped by 13.5% to a total of 14.4 million, and the source of much of this growth was the increase in the number of very-low-income, single-parent families. On the other hand, net new federal commitments to provide assisted (or subsidized) housing averaged a little more than 100,000 units in the period 1988–1995, down from 300,000 to 400,000 units in the late 1970s; moreover, 1996 marked the first time in the history of federal housing programs that the number of assisted units actually fell (Joint Center for Housing Studies, 1995, 1997). In most major cities, the waiting lists for Section 8 housing subsidy and public housing units stretch for years. The number of low-cost unsubsidized rental units has also declined below 1974 levels, which is inevitable given that between 1973 and 1983 alone, the United States permanently lost some 4.5 million affordable rental units through demolition or structural conversion to higher-priced housing (U.S. House of Representatives, 1990).

The mismatch between the decreasing supply of affordable low-income rental housing units and the increasing demand for these units, attributable to the increasing numbers of poor households and the erosion of real incomes among such households, has been proven by many studies to be the primary cause of homelessness in many cities (McChesney, 1990; Ringheim, 1993; Shinn & Gillespie, 1994). In Ringheim's (1993) study of Houston between 1976 and 1983, rents increased far in excess of inflation, whereas renter incomes stagnated, a pattern that explained increasing vulnerability to homelessness among extremely poor minority (especially black) households with children, even in the midst of massive vacancies in rental housing units. An analysis of 482 New York City families who were newly homeless showed that nearly half of them (43%) had been primary tenants in their own living quarters in the year prior to the shelter request and that 47% of the primary tenants had left their residence due to eviction/rent problems (Weitzman, Knickman, & Shinn, 1990).

Because of the tight low-income rental market, the failure rates of rental-assistance vouchers or certificates (the number of households failing to find affordable housing even with a voucher or certificate) reached 50% to 60% in big cities in the 1980s (U.S. House of Representatives, 1990). In 1993 only 26% of very-low-income renter households lived in federally assisted housing (Dolbeare, 1996). In spite of some preventive measures in the 1990 Cranston–Gonzalez National Affordable Housing Act (PL 101–625), tens of thousands of subsidized rental housing stocks will be lost as the federal contract with private developers runs out in coming years.

In recent years, we have also witnessed the loss of valuable public housing stock through demolition, sales, and voluntary or mandatory conversion to commercial purposes. Although the environmental problems of some public housing projects render their demolition inevitable, demolitions and conversions of public housing units accompanied by inadequate relocation assistance have often displaced thousands of low-income residents. Moreover, between fiscal year 1995 and fiscal year 1997, in response to the tremendous pressure to downsize federal agencies and cut domestic discretionary funding, the Department of Housing and Urban Development (HUD) budget overall was slashed by 25% and that for public housing was cut 20%, from nearly $8 billion to just over $6 billion. Modernization funds took the biggest hit, and operating subsidies, while level-funded, continue to provide only 85% of what is needed under the Performance Funding System (PFS) (NLIHC, 1997). Given the large backlog of buildings needing rehabilitation in many projects, the budget cut is likely to further delay the admission of those on waiting lists. Thus, in the absence of major public policy changes regarding low-income housing, the housing-affordability crisis and the gross human suffering we have seen in the plight of the homeless will continue to affect tens of thousands of poor families with children.

Poor single mothers who lack education and job skills often depend on public assistance as a major income source. But the real dollar value of Aid to Families with Dependent Children (AFDC) had declined by almost half since the mid-1970s, and, in 1995, not a single state paid benefits high enough to allow them to reach even 75% of the poverty line. The increasing rent burden borne by these poor single mothers on welfare has indicated that affordability problems are disproportionately visited upon them and that these problems may have been especially severe in situations where they had compounding physical and/or mental health problems to deal with. The 1996 welfare reform that replaced AFDC, an entitlement program, with Temporary Assistance to Needy Families (TANF), a block grant to each state with a stipulated 5-year lifetime limit for welfare receipt, poses a new threat. Fortunately, the currently strong job market may make it possible for many welfare recipients to make the transition from welfare to work. But for those with limited education and skills, the transition may be difficult. Even if they succeed in securing employment, they are not likely to earn enough to afford rent for decent housing and their other living expenses.

Many states are still in the beginning stage of implementing their own new welfare or welfare-to-work programs, and thus it is too early to assess the real impact of the welfare reform on the lives of poor families. Some states appear committed to helping poor parents achieve self-sufficiency with an array of supportive services, including subsidized child care, health care, and transportation, whereas others appear to have become more punitive than assistive. The extremely poor households headed by young, single females dependent either on insufficient welfare benefits and the vagaries of the welfare bureaucracy or on low-paying, unstable jobs as their primary or sole source of income can be easily thrown into homelessness out of already precarious housing situations. Unless each state combines job training and placement with generous earnings disregard, many more poor women with limited or no marketable skills may end up homeless after the 5-year (shorter in many states) lifetime limit.

Urban Decline, Spatial Isolation of Poor Minorities, and Substandard Housing

Increasing numbers of households headed by young, black, single women along with the concentration of poverty and the crisis of housing affordability among black families are the logical consequences of the social and economic marginalization of central cities and the spatial segregation of poor blacks in dilapidated inner-city neighborhoods where the tax base, quality of public schools, and availability of social services are all declining. Wilson (1987, 1996) has powerfully illustrated the deindustrialization that took away well-paid manufacturing and other low-skilled jobs from cities, especially from many inner-city neighborhoods. Over the past few decades, the demand for poorly educated labor has declined markedly while the demand for workers with higher education (e.g., high-tech information-processing white-collar jobs) has increased substantially. Because of their lack of education, many poor blacks in central cities have not been able to gain access to these well-paid jobs (Kasarda, 1989; Wilson, 1987, 1996). Even minimum-wage jobs that do not require much education have become less accessible to poor urban blacks, who seldom have private means of transportation, because most, if not all, of these jobs have moved to suburbs. According to Wilson (1996), in the period 1987–1989, a low-skilled male worker was jobless 8 1/2 weeks longer than he would have been in 1967–1969. The proportion of men who permanently dropped out of the labor force was also more than twice as high in the late 1980s as it was in the 1960s.

Wilson showed that increased joblessness among young black males over the past decades was positively correlated with the increased numbers of single-female-headed families, because the high rate of joblessness means the number of potential marriage partners who can afford raising a family has declined. At the same time that the number of employment opportunities available to low-skilled males was declining, the age of sexual maturity and the initiation of sexual activity dropped considerably, exposing more young women to the risk of early pregnancy (Rossi, 1994). Also, poor educational preparation and long-term poverty often breed attitudes of fatalism, powerlessness, and hopelessness among young men and women. On top of these attitudes, the reality of their dim prospects for the future is not a good incentive for young men and women to postpone sexual activities and child bearing (Joint Economic Committee, 1992).

In the post-Fordist society, which is characterized by technological change, internationalization (or globalization) of economy, concentration of ownership of businesses, and centralization of control (Marcuse, 1996), business-led efforts to contain wages of low-skilled, service-sector jobs have also contributed to the precipitous drop in real income among low-income workers and to increasing income polarization. That is, owing to the recovering economy in 1994 and 1995, the unemployment rates have fallen to the lowest levels in many years. Nevertheless, the economic status of those in the lower strata has not changed much relative to those in the higher strata. That is, the average incomes received by the lowest 20% of households were $8,301 in 1980 and $8,350 in 1995, whereas those received by the highest 20% were $85,279 in 1980 and $109,411 in 1995 (all in 1995 dollars). During the same period, the average incomes received by the top 5% changed from $123,359 to $188,828, a 53% increase (Concord Coalition, 1997).

More importantly, the ripple of the recovering economy has not yet reached the racially segregated urban fringe areas where the "ghetto poor" are concentrated; in reality, the economic boom is most likely to bypass these areas, because their ties to the mainstream of economic life is tenuous at best with few jobs, services, and cultural resources. "The economic marginality of the ghetto poor is cruelly reinforced, therefore, by conditions in the neighborhoods in which they live" (Wilson, 1996, p. 54). The residents of these racial-geographic areas who can make it out into the world are more likely to leave for a better environment than to stay with those who cannot make it. After more than two decades of exodus by the better off, the areas remain isolated and abandoned from the rest of society through recession or downturns and prosperity or upturns in economy. In other words, "the post-Fordist ghetto is a 'new ghetto' in that it has become an outcast ghetto, a ghetto of the excluded, rather than more generally of the dominated and exploited, or of the marginal" (Marcuse, 1996, p. 179).

Massey, Gross, and Shibuya (1994) confirmed that industrial changes and the outmigration of middle-class blacks and whites to the suburbs were indeed responsible for the residential segregation of poor blacks in central cities in the early 1970s. But Massey et al. also showed that in later years, racial discrimination in housing markets was a more powerful force that isolated blacks economically and socially and contributed to the concentration of poverty in black neighborhoods. That is, because of racial discrimination, both nonpoor and poor blacks moving out of a poor black neighborhood had a much higher probability of moving into another poor black neighborhood than into a nonpoor neighborhood, black or white. Poor blacks, especially, tend to gravitate from one poor black neighborhood to another, without much possibility of leaving these economically depressed and dilapidated areas. So the vicious cycle of joblessness, single parenthood, poverty, and welfare dependency continues. In the absence of any spatial and economic policies that would systematically reduce the social and economic deprivation of poor urban blacks, their plight has been worsening.

Concentration of poverty also implies a simultaneous concentration of crime, violence, family disruption, and educational failure (Massey, 1994; Massey et al., 1994). The disappearance of businesses—as sources of legitimate economic activity—has stimulated the influx of drugs and criminal activities (see Wacquant & Wilson, 1989; Wilson, 1996). For lack of other employment opportunities, working for drug dealers has become the only employment opportunity, albeit in the black market, among many youths in poor racially and spatially segregated neighborhoods. Wanting even basic cultural, social, and recreational services, the youths also join gangs, which have become major social organizations. Especially since the early 1980s, when crack cocaine became widely marketed on many streets of poor inner-city neighborhoods, the terribly addictive power of this illegal substance has been a cause of increasingly violent crimes and has further exacerbated isolation, social disintegration, and condemnation of these neighborhoods. These violent neighborhoods and their residents have indeed become outcasts of society.

The victims of the most sinister effects of substance abuse and violence are the poor who live in the neighborhoods. The lives of poor women and children, especially, are constantly threatened by the random crime and violence that accompany drug trafficking on the streets and spill over into residential and school buildings. Domestic violence, also a frequent deadly side effect of substance abuse, disintegrates families and traumatizes women and children both physically and mentally.

As these extremely harsh and disadvantaged neighborhood conditions are not conducive to maintaining even a minimal level of housing quality, they put much of the rental stock now occupied by low-income households at risk of loss. Although poor renters may pay a high share of their income for rent, their payments are generally insufficient to properly maintain old units (Joint Center for Housing Studies, 1995). Because of this problem as well as the falling property values that accompany escalating violence and worsening economic situations in the neighborhoods, owners of rental units in poor neighborhoods often disinvest in the properties and foreclose/abandon units (Timmer, Eitzen, & Talley, 1994). It is an irony that boarded-up houses and abandoned buildings have become increasingly common fixtures of central city landscapes at a time when increasing numbers of poor families are looking for shelter.

Because investment in the upkeep of rental units is often inadequate and landlords refuse to fix the problems, poor families in central cities often live in substandard units. They are also more likely than nonpoor families to live in housing that is deficient since they are unable to afford decent housing. In its periodic reports to Congress, HUD documents the dramatic growth of renter households with "worst-case needs"— unsubsidized renter households that have incomes below 50% of area median and pay more than half of their income for housing costs and/ or live in structurally inadequate units. Between 1974 and 1995 the number of households having worst-case needs increased by two thirds to 6 million. Of these 6 million very-low-income renters, 1.3 million, or 22%, were living in structurally inadequate housing (Joint Center for Housing Studies, 1997). The HUD study also found that minority households are much more likely to live in structurally inadequate housing than white households; some 20.2% of very-low-income blacks and 14.3% of very-low-income Hispanics, as compared to 10.1% of their white counterparts, lived in inadequate housing. These relatively large shares reflect the concentration of inadequate housing in inner cities and nonmetro areas—communities where minority households tend to live (Joint Center for Housing Studies, 1997).

Despite the direct relationship between housing and the changing structure of the urban economy, however, there has been an almost complete absence of concerted efforts to revitalize inner cities in the

1980s and 1990s. The past two decades can indeed be characterized by "bipartisan federal disengagement from the cities," and urban policy under the Reagan and Bush administrations relied heavily upon economic development shaped by private investment decisions and a tax reform package that required state and local governments to raise more of their own revenues to deal with problems in cities (Ames et al., 1992, pp. 208–209). The status of central cities has continued to decline under the Clinton administration, with its sole program aimed at helping American cities, "empowerment zones," but an empty slogan (Fainstein & Fainstein, 1995).

The drug-related violence and crime that ravage the streets of poor inner-city neighborhoods also drive some poor families with children out to homelessness, as parents flee to a temporary shelter, abandoning their home in fear for their children's safety. Interviews with 100 homeless women with children staying in shelters in Richmond, Virginia, identified excessive drug use and vandalism in the neighborhood as a reason for homelessness (Khanna, Singh, Nemil, Best, & Ellis, 1992). Yet the link between crime and violence in the poor inner-city neighborhoods and homelessness among poor women and children has been ignored in many studies.

On top of crime and violence, the physical dilapidation of some units has reached a point that threatens these families' daily survival. Children become sick in unheated, roach- and rodent-infested apartment buildings, poisoned by lead in old paint, and injured by building fires caused by leaking gas and exposed wires. Weitzman et al.'s (1990) study of a sample of 482 New York City families with children who were newly homeless in 1988 shows that 18% of the families who had been primary tenants in their own apartment cited building problems as their reason for leaving their housing. Because of the crushing effects of poverty, rent burdens, physical inadequacy of housing, and dangerous neighborhoods, many families in central cities are at risk of becoming homeless even if they are not currently so.

Unlike unattached homeless adults, homeless families seldom spend nights on the streets. Upon becoming homeless, many families double up with relatives or friends until they have overstayed their welcome, and then they go to family shelters. There most of them are helped to find housing. But lack of a private vehicle, limited welfare grants/earnings, and racial discrimination in housing markets usually send these families back to the same depressed poor black neighborhoods from which they came and in which they are likely to go through a revolving door of homelessness. Once they become homeless, the families also often face barriers of antichild and anti–welfare recipient discrimination in the private housing market and the difficulty of accumulating "first, last, and deposit" (the first and last months' rent and the deposit that must be paid up front) (Rosenthal, 1994).)

The most effective prevention of repeated homelessness among vulnerable families is to provide dwellings that are decent and affordable, such as subsidized or public housing in safe neighborhoods. A follow-up study of formerly homeless families in St. Louis found that families who received a Section 8 placement were much less likely to become homeless again than those who did not (Stretch & Kreuger, 1992). Research on 169 formerly homeless families in New York City also found that the type and quality of the new housing and the families' comfort level in their new neighborhoods were among the strongest predictors of who would become homeless again. Once families had subsidized housing and income support from welfare, case management services made only a small difference (Weitzman & Berry, 1994; cited in Shinn & Weitzman, 1996). Another study found that, when asked about how they had been able to get out of homelessness, formerly homeless families said they had been helped most by an increase in income, the support of family and friends, and access to affordable housing (Dornbusch, 1993). These findings underscore the significance of poverty, rent burden, and housing environment as the primary reasons for homelessness and repeated homelessness among families.

Mental Illness, Drug Abuse, and Domestic Abuse

(As mentioned, homeless mothers are more likely to have had a history of hospitalization for mental illness than are poor housed mothers, but the rates are far lower than those for homeless individuals, both men and women, unaccompanied by children.)A study of 677 New York City mothers who requested shelter and 495 poor housed mothers showed that only 4% of the former and 0.8% of the latter had ever experienced psychiatric hospitalization (Weitzman et al., 1992). Studies based on probability or nonprobability samples of homeless sheltered mothers in different locations (Bassuk & Rosenberg, 1988; Burt & Cohen, 1989) may show rates of psychiatric hospitalizations or prevalence of mental illness a little higher than those found by Weitzman et al.'s study.

If there were enough affordable housing, mental illness of a mother/father alone would not force families onto streets or into shelters. Few studies of homeless families attribute homelessness directly to a mother's preexisting mental disorder. It appears that mothers with severe mental illness lost custody of their children because of their inability to take care of them before they became homeless. Mothers accompanied by children are thus not likely to become homeless solely or primarily because of mental disorder. However, because of the shortage of affordable low-income housing and the resulting competition for it among the poor, the mentally ill are more likely to lose out in the competition and be vulnerable to homelessness than the poor who do not have such a disability.

A very serious problem with the mental health of homeless mothers and children is that their homeless experiences are likely to not only exacerbate existing disorders but also cause all sorts of emotional distresses, notably depression and anxiety, which may interfere with normal daily functioning. Without adequate supportive services, many homeless families may thus have a tougher time coping with homelessness along with impaired mental and emotional status.

With respect to substance abuse, most studies with comparison groups reported drug abuse 2 to 8 times higher among homeless than among housed mothers, with the prevalence rates among homeless mothers fluctuating between 8% and 50% (see McChesney, 1995). (The wide range may be due to the fact that most studies of homeless families are based on those staying in temporary shelters, some of which do not admit mothers with substance abuse problems.) Unlike psychiatric disorders, drug abuse may have led some families to homelessness, because the habit eats up money that would otherwise be available for paying rent. Even when a substance abuse problem was caused by the family's friends or relatives who shared housing with them, the family's risk of homelessness was elevated (Weitzman et al., 1992).

Many poor mothers who have lived most of their lives in poor inner-city neighborhoods are easy prey to the rampant crack epidemics in them. Even those who resisted were at high risk for being in a relationship with a substance abuser. In a study of 80 homeless mothers in Massachusetts shelters, more than 40% of the women reported that their most recent boyfriend or spouse was a substance abuser (Bassuk, 1992). When the man's alcohol or drug abuse problem spirals out of control, the woman usually leaves the relationship to avoid the physical abuse that usually accompanies substance abuse problems. These women may double up with friends or relatives for a while, eventually ending up in homeless shelters. But homeless mothers often lack the social support that others can rely upon in times of hardship: Either their parents are dead, their parents and siblings do not live in the same geographic area, or they are estranged from their parents and siblings (Bassuk, 1990). Even parents and/or siblings who are willing to help are often in no position to do so, due to their own poverty and overcrowding (Rossi, 1994).

Most studies report that homeless mothers are significantly more likely to have been abused as both children and adults than are housed poor mothers (see McChesney, 1995). Other studies found no such difference, although both groups reported relatively high levels of child-hood physical or sexual abuse (Bassuk et al., 1997; Goodman, 1991). Bassuk et al.'s (1997) study of homeless and housed poor mothers in Worcester County, Massachusetts, found that 19.6% of homeless mothers, in contrast to 8.3% of poor housed mothers, had lived in foster care as children. (The Institute for Children and Poverty's study of homeless mothers in New York City also found that 20% had lived in foster care as children [daCosta Nunez, 1994].) In addition to foster care placement, Bassuk et al. (1997) found that a respondent's mother's drug use (12.3% of homeless mothers, in comparison to 3.7% of housed poor mothers) was a childhood risk factor.

With respect to the homeless mothers' victimization as adults, there is consistent evidence that they were more likely to have been battered than were housed poor mothers (see McChesney, 1993). As mentioned, it is estimated that 25% to 35% of homeless mothers became homeless by fleeing domestic violence. Again, there are different assessments of the role of domestic violence in precipitating homelessness among poor women. Some studies (Hagen, 1987; Zorza, 1991) reported that domestic violence is a leading cause of homelessness among women with children. But Bassuk's (1992) and Weitzman et al.'s (1992) studies report that, despite the high incidence of past victimization among homeless moth-ers, domestic violence only infrequently precipitated the current epi-sode of homelessness. These different assessments may result from the fact that some studies included but others excluded battered women's shelters. Studies that did not include these shelters may have under-counted battered women who became homeless (Steinbock, 1995). The insignificance of domestic violence history in the presence of economic status variables in the multivariate modeling of housing status (Bassuk et al., 1996) supports the likelihood that domestic violence combined with poverty rather than domestic violence alone is a leading cause of homelessness.

Minority women and women living in poverty are at especially high risk of victimization by violence because they experience much higher rates of frequent, uncontrollable, and threatening life events than the general population (Browne, 1993). Urban decline, joblessness, poverty, drug and alcohol problems, and frequent family disruptions inevitably expose residents of most, if not all, ghettos to violence by strangers as well as by family members and friends. For poor minority mothers who lack economic independence and are virtually imprisoned by their environment, "opportunities for improvement of living conditions or escape from threatening situations may be severely limited, and the level of protective resources is typically low" (Browne, 1993, p. 371). When these poor women and their children are forced to leave their housing to escape abuse and possible death, more often than not, they have nowhere safe to go and end up in a shelter. Thus, domestic violence is definitely a contributing cause of homelessness for many families, and the relationship between domestic violence, poverty, and urban decline must not be forgotten.

EFFECTS OF HOMELESSNESS ON FAMILIES

The lives of homeless families exiled in drug-infested welfare hotels or in temporary shelters of large cities, and the physical and mental price they pay for being homeless, have not been described as extensively as have either the circumstances that led to their homelessness or their sociodemographic characteristics. The subjects of in-depth qualitative interviews with homeless people were mostly unattached individuals (see Butler, 1994; Liebow, 1993; Passaro, 1996; Rosenthal, 1994; Rossi, 1989). Only a few books (Kozol, 1988; Rosenthal, 1994; Timmer et al., 1994) described, through extensive contacts, how homeless families suffer from and cope with homelessness. Several other studies based on in-depth qualitative interviews with or participant observations of homeless mothers and children provide occasional windows through which we can catch glimpses of their lives (Bassuk & Gallagher, 1990; Baumann, 1993; Berck, 1992; Boxill & Beaty, 1990; McChesney, 1992). Most other studies of the effects of homelessness focus on children and are based on quantitative analyses of data on academic performance and on physical and psychological health. However, the pain and suffering faced by homeless parents, especially single mothers, as providers for and protectors of their children have yet to be documented and understood. In the following pages, we review existing literature on the effects of homelessness on families and children.

Effects of Homelessness on Parents

Food, shelter, and clothing are basic human rights and necessities for a bare minimum standard of living. Deprivation of one or more of these basic necessities disrupts normal physical and emotional functioning. For a family, the loss of a shelter can cause especially serious problems, because, more often than not, it also entails hunger and inadequate clothing. Loss of a home means the loss of most of the family's other belongings. The feeling of uprootedness, grief for a lost home, and the lack of the sense of security provided by having one's own home may also engender depression and anxiety even among the most resilient, impairing their ability to function normally. Once they become homeless, families face enormous difficulties in conducting their daily lives as usual. Doubling up with relatives or friends who themselves are often poor and dwell in already crowded housing units can be an extremely depressive and aggravating experience (see McChesney, 1992). For most homeless families, doubled-up living arrangements result in friction among and estrangement from those in their precious small social support networks and turn out to be temporary and transient. Likewise, it is downright impossible to have an orderly life in a welfare hotel without cooking facilities but with illicit drug traffic or in a temporary shelter where families are required to take their meager belongings and vacate the premises during the day (because shelter staff are volunteers who have daytime jobs). Lack of privacy and being subject to the rules that need to be followed in congregate living environments can be nerve-racking for both parents and children. The physical experience of a whole family's being compacted in a small space can be stifling and literally create breathing problems among both adults and children (Kozol, 1988).

Homelessness often causes family disruption, with separation between husband and wife as well as between parents and children. Some shelters may not admit all the family members because of a lack of space. Other family shelters bar men (sometimes including preteen or teenage boys) from staying with their female relatives and children, sending them to different shelters for homeless men or placing the adolescents in foster care. Studies also show that an increasing number of children were separated from their parents and placed in foster care solely or primarily because their families were homeless or living in inadequate or unsafe housing. Parents' lack of adequate housing was a major reason for placement of black children in 30% of the foster care cases studied (U.S. House of Representatives, 1990).

Even if parents and children manage to stay together, the disruptive and traumatizing experience of homelessness impairs parental functioning. Most mothers are overwhelmed and depressed about being homeless and often have little energy left to care for their children consistently (Bassuk & Gallagher, 1990). When families are forced to cope with a myriad of crises on a daily basis, parents' capacity to provide protection and support and to respond to their children's needs may be eroded (Hausman & Hammen, 1993). When a family is placed in a temporary shelter and must share space with other families in a congregate living situation, the previously private interaction between the mother and her children is affected by its public and often scrutinized nature and is externally controlled by others, creating a sense of powerlessness in the mother: "The traditional role of mother as provider, family leader, organizer and standard setter was experienced by mothers as having vanished" (Boxill & Beaty, 1990, p. 60). Someone else decides when, what, and where the family will eat, wash up, and rest.

A study of the meaning of the homeless experience, as lived by 15 homeless mothers in shelters, reveals these women's fatigue and despair, diminished self-respect, frustration from lack of control over their lives, yearnings for privacy and stability, and struggle to maintain boundaries and a sense of connectedness (Baumann, 1993). The loss of a home brought these women chaos, uncertainty, and insecurity. Although shelters were safer than the places where some of these women had previously lived, most of them did not experience them as places where they could rest and feel safe. With the experience of many day-to-day indignities, the pressure to adapt to institutional rules and regulations, and the decreasing hope of getting a place of their own, the women expressed the meaning of homelessness as a whirlpool or downward spiral (Baumann, 1993, pp. 67–68).

As mentioned, most homeless parents have been receiving welfare and/or working in a low-paying job prior to their becoming homeless. Because public assistance benefits are not intended to raise a family's standard of living above the poverty line and even full-time minimum-wage workers cannot lift a family above the poverty line, these parents have been living on the edge, constantly struggling to make ends meet (see Rank, 1994). The amount of income received each month is simply not enough to cover even bare minimum necessities, and trying to lead a normal life under this severe economic constraint is extremely frustrating. Yet becoming homeless may well be the worst of all consequences of poverty, and the pain and frustration of homeless parents may reflect the harshest of all crises in their lives.

Effects of Homelessness on Children

Even before they became homeless, children often had had a variety of developmental and health problems that were mostly ascribable to extreme poverty. Poor children often face multiple risk factors such as hunger, an unhealthy and transient housing environment, uneducated parents, and high exposure to stressful life events, including family breakups, domestic abuse, and neighborhood violence (Masten, 1992; McChesney, 1993). The poverty-stricken and violence-laden neighborhoods in which they live are not conducive to their healthy and normal development. Poor single mothers have only limited resources to provide for their children and limited access to preventive—including prenatal—and curative health care. But loss of a home, the discontinuity of place of residence, and all other hardships that accompany homelessness can traumatize these poor children, exacerbating existing problems and creating a whole new set of them. Congregate and unsanitary living conditions in shelters put children at higher risk for the rapid spread of infectious and communicable diseases. Once they become sick, they do not find an adequate curative environment in the crowded living conditions of the shelters and welfare hotels. Although some family shelters provide basic in-house health care services or refer families to ones outside, preventive health care for children whose families move about frequently is still very inadequate not only because of accessibility problems but also because of the families' very instability. Health problems caused by dietary insufficiency, such as malnutrition, anemia, and overweight, are also more common among homeless children than children in the general population (see Burg, 1994).

Studies have consistently found that homeless children are more often ill than their domiciled counterparts and that they suffer from both acute and chronic illnesses, especially upper respiratory disorders (including asthma), minor skin diseases, ear disorders, gastrointestinal problems, trauma, eye disorders, and infestations of lice (McNamee, Bartek, & Lynes, 1994; Wright, 1990, 1991). Compared to poor housed children, homeless children also have higher rates of other poverty-related problems, including delayed immunizations, elevated lead levels, and iron deficiencies, which may be related to other unmeasured nutritional deficiencies (Bernstein, Alperstein, & Fierman, 1988, as quoted in Rafferty & Shinn, 1991). Children who are homeless and/or born to homeless women are at high risk from the effects of their mother's and their own inadequate diets (Shane, 1996). Feeding children nutritionally balanced meals is a difficult task when the family lives in a welfare hotel without any cooking facility or in a temporary shelter that does not have a large operational budget.

Studies also report that a majority of homeless preschool children exhibit developmental delays. The behaviors most frequently mentioned include short attention spans, withdrawal, aggression, speech

delays, sleep disorders, regressive behaviors, and immature motor behavior (Rafferty & Shinn, 1991). A study of homeless children in Massachusetts shelters reported that 47% of the preschoolers had at least
one developmental delay and that their average score on the Simmons
Behavior Checklist was significantly higher than the average scores for
normal and emotionally disturbed children (Bassuk & Rubin, 1987).

Studies comparing homeless preschool children with their poor
housed peers also indicate that homeless children have more cognitive
and emotional problems. One study of children in Boston shelters
showed that 54% of the homeless preschoolers, as opposed to 16% of
their poor housed peers, manifested at least one major developmental
lag, measured by the Denver Developmental Screening Test, although
the two groups were similar in scores on the Simmons Behavior Checklist (Bassuk & Rosenberg, 1990). Another comparison between preschool children residing in city shelters and their poor housed peers
showed that the homeless children exhibited slower development and
more emotional-behavioral problems (Rescorla, Parker, & Stolley, 1991).
DiBiase and Waddell's (1995) study of preschoolers participating in
Head Start programs also found that homeless children showed significantly more problem behaviors, including symptoms of depression,
social withdrawal, and schizoid behavior, than housed children. Moreover, homeless children generally perceived themselves as being less
cognitively, socially, and physically competent as well as less well accepted by their mothers than did housed children. Teachers also rated
homeless children as being less cognitively competent than housed
children, but rated the two groups similarly on peer relations and physical competence (DiBiase & Waddell, 1995).

Studies comparing school-age homeless children and their poor
housed peers show mixed results. Ziesemer, Marcoux, and Marwell's
(1994) study reported that previously homeless children were similar
to those children whose families were low income and frequently moved
about in academic performance, adaptive functioning, and problem behaviors, although both groups had substantially more problems than
the norm. Academically, almost two thirds of both groups were below
their grade level. Rescorla et al. (1991) reported that homeless school-
age children scored significantly lower than their poor housed peers
in vocabulary scores, but that the two groups did not differ significantly
in their block design and reading scores, although the latter scored
somewhat higher. The homeless children were not significantly different
from the poor housed children in behavior problems. Zima, Wells, and
Freeman's (1994) study of 169 homeless school-age children in Los
Angeles and Whitman, Accardo, Boyert, and Kendagor's (1990) study

of homeless children in a St. Louis shelter also found their language and reading skills were severely delayed. A study of educational achievement of 59 African-American and 10 Native American children recently homeless also found that the standardized individual achievement test scores of 80% of the African-American children fell in the bottom quartile and that 20% had repeated a grade. Of the Native American children, 7 scored at age and grade level and 1 had repeated a grade. For children who had academic difficulty, teachers also reported significant problems in behavior and adaptive functioning, indicating intercorrelation between academic and behavior problems (Masten et al., 1997).

The dislocation of children from their communities and their subsequent bouncing between shelters often require them to transfer into new schools (Rafferty, 1995). Children also skip school for lack of transportation to a new school, lack of proper school clothing (especially in areas with harsh winters) and needed supplies, lack of immunization records, and bureaucratic problems that delay the transfer of school records or even lose them entirely (Dupper & Halter, 1994; Rafferty, 1995). Despite the 1990 federal mandate to remove the residency requirement in the best interest of homeless children, some states continue to impose the requirement in a manner that bars them from attending either the school in their area of origin or the school in the area in which the shelter is located (Rafferty, 1995).

Due to crowded and noisy conditions at shelters, children's sleep may be disrupted, which, combined with hunger, leads to fatigue and to diminished attention span and tolerance levels in school (Shane, 1996). At the shelter, children lack quiet space to do their homework, and their parents may be too tired or distracted to help them with it. On top of the emotional trauma of being homeless and the multiple developmental and health problems that predate their homelessness, these children are too often put at a serious academic disadvantage by having their education interrupted by such obstacles. Thus, it is not unexpected that a majority of school-age homeless, previously homeless, and poor mobile children are required to repeat grades and/or are failing or performing below-average work. If homelessness and transient and unstable living situations continue over an extended period, the children may be precluded from remediation and catching up.

Considering that homeless children have gone through negative life changes, including the major loss of a home and separation from loved ones, friends, and a familiar environment, it is not surprising that the majority of them suffer from severe anxiety and depression, as measured by the Children's Manifest Anxiety Scale and the Children's Depression Inventory (Bassuk & Rosenberg, 1990; Bassuk & Rubin, 1987; Wagner &

Menke, 1991; Zima et al., 1994). In Bassuk and Rubin's study, a majority of school-age homeless children said that they thought about killing themselves but they would not. The acute stress associated with being homeless also contributes to children's depression. Moreover, children who have witnessed domestic violence involving a parent and lost a home are likely to exhibit even more intensified posttraumatic stress disorder (PTSD) symptomatology. A recent study indicated a significant association between status as a witness to domestic violence and PTSD diagnosis among children ages 6 through 12 years (Kilpatrick, Litt, & Williams, 1997). Nevertheless, only a minority of children had ever received psychiatric evaluation, to say nothing of treatment, because their parents lacked awareness of the children's problems and, in any case, had not had access to community mental health clinics if they had wanted to seek treatment for them (Zima et al., 1994).

Given these multiple barriers to proper cognitive and emotional development, homeless children face a severely compromised future. Lack of a protective environment and the resulting sense of insecurity, with loss of feelings of self-control and self-efficacy, can lead to states of passivity and learned helplessness, especially as the chaos and environmental insults persist over time (Donahue & Tuber, 1995). Most homeless children are not able to stave off the trauma of living in overcrowded emergency shelters or violence-ridden welfare hotels, and "visions of academic achievement or career aspirations tend to get overshadowed by the harsh realities they face daily" (Donahue & Tuber, 1995, p. 251). All these children might well be gifted, but living in an environment that does not satisfy even their basic survival needs prevents them from achieving their potential. Thus, the primary victims of homelessness are innocent children, who are crushed, physically and emotionally, by the weight of the trauma of homelessness and are unable to transcend the negative environment.

POLICIES AND PROGRAMS FOR HOMELESS FAMILIES WITH CHILDREN

Policy Responses

In 1987, triggered by widespread homelessness, the Stewart B. McKinney Homeless Assistance Act (PL 100–77) was passed with broad bipartisan support. To date, it remains the only major federal legislative response to homelessness. The McKinney Act was expressly designed to be only a first, emergency response to homelessness and to meet the "critically urgent" needs of the nation's homeless (Foscarinis, 1996; U.S. House of Representatives, 1993). As originally enacted, this omnibus act includes the following titles:

Title I includes a statement of six findings by Congress regarding the problems of homelessness, purpose of the act, and definition of "homeless individual."

Title II establishes the Interagency Council on Homelessness as an independent entity within the executive branch of the federal government, with the responsibility of preparing an annual report to the president and to Congress on the needs of homeless people, federal government activities, and recommendations.

Title III authorizes and defines the emergency food and shelter grants programs within the Federal Emergency Management Agency (FEMA).

Title IV focuses on HUD-administered emergency shelters, transitional/supportive housing, and a small program for permanent SRO.

Title V specifies identification and use of surplus federal property to be made available for use in assisting the homeless.

Title VI establishes a grant program for public and private nonprofit organizations to provide for the delivery of health services to homeless individuals.

Title VII creates programs for the education of homeless adults and children, job training, and community services.

Title VIII establishes food assistance for the homeless through the Food Stamp program and the Temporary Emergency Food Assistance program.

Title IX requires the Veterans Administration to fund the conversion of surplus space in VA hospitals and health facilities to provide beds for homeless veterans.

Since its enactment, the McKinney Act has been amended several times to make it more responsive to increasing problems of homelessness and to add new provisions, such as Shelter Plus Care for homeless persons with disabilities, and to expand and strengthen such existing provisions as the education of homeless children and youth. In general, the amendments to the McKinney Act have emphasized longer-term solutions, including eviction prevention, permanent housing, and employment opportunities (Foscarinis, 1995). However, some other significant provisions have been defunded in recent years. One notable change was with the Interagency Council on Homelessness, which had been created by Title II. Under President Bill Clinton, the council was charged with developing federal strategies to break the cycle of homelessness. The council proposed a continuum-of-care approach, which was borrowed from the mental health field. Under this approach, local boards, with financial support from HUD, were supposed to provide a set of services ranging from shelters and mental health and substance abuse services to permanent housing and strategies to prevent homelessness (Johnson & Cnaan, 1995; U.S. Department of Housing and Urban Development, 1994). But in 1994 the council was defunded and made part of the White House Domestic Council, and starting with fiscal year 1995, the programs were funded from HUD's operations budget (Hombs, 1994). To date, however, local boards have not materialized, and the effectiveness of the council in carrying out its responsibility for providing a federal forum and coordinating 18 federal agencies to combat homelessness has not yet been proven.

In fiscal year 1998, $1.14 billion was appropriated under the McKinney Act to fund HUD homeless-assistance programs ($823 million), emergency food and shelter programs ($100 million), health care for the homeless ($71 million), projects for assistance in transition from homelessness ($23 million), education for homeless children and youth ($28.8 million), runaway and homeless youth programs ($58.6 million), and homeless veterans reintegration programs ($3 million). (No funding has been earmarked for adult education for the homeless since 1996.) The 1998 level of total funding is similar to those in fiscal years 1996 and 1997, but it represents a 25% reduction from the fiscal year 1995 funding level. Under these programs, the federal government distributes funds to eligible grantees (states, territories, large cities, and urban communities). Funding for some programs, such as that for emergency shelter grants, is distributed to these grantees on a formula basis with a matching requirement. The current distribution system can be identified as a modified block grant, because decision making and priority setting occur at the local level.

Since its passage, the programs funded under the McKinney Act have provided important emergency measures to address some of the most urgent needs of the homeless: emergency shelter and food, health and mental health care, children's education, transitional housing, job training, and other support services. For the past 10 years, antihomeless activities by most state and local governments and private nonprofit organizations have been direct results of the McKinney Act fiscal incentives and planning requirements (Watson, 1996). Unfortunately, however, most programs funded by the McKinney Act were meant only as short-term, emergency responses and were directed at ameliorating or managing symptoms instead of ending homelessness by addressing systemic causes of homelessness, poverty, and the lack of low-income affordable housing. As shown by the dollar amount, a large share of the funding under the McKinney Act is still aimed at providing emergency shelters, transitional housing, and temporary services for the homeless.

As indicated, Title IV of the McKinney Act includes a small program for permanent SRO housing. It also includes small preventive measures in the form of financial assistance to families facing eviction or termination of utility services. In October 1997 President Clinton signed into law H.R. 680, a bill that would allow unused federal property to be made available for permanent housing for low-income persons for less than the prevailing market price, which amounts to a major revamping of Title V with an emphasis on permanent housing. Other than these, the act has done little to address the fundamental problems of the low-income housing market and the provision of permanent housing to the homeless. Instead of encouraging construction and rehabilitation of low-income housing units, opening them to homeless and other low-income people, the McKinney Act is still geared primarily to funding emergency relief. This is a sign that policy and lawmakers are still treating homelessness more as a personal responsibility than as a systemic issue, despite the massive increase in homelessness across the country. In other words, this law is a notable example of federal policies and programs that continue to treat homelessness and the problems it brings as emergencies. These emergency-relief efforts no doubt alleviate the suffering of the homeless, but they also tend to be "ad hoc, stopgap policies dealing, for the most part, only with manifestations of the problems" and to divert resources from long-term and fundamental solutions (Lipsky & Smith, 1989, p. 6).

The current funding level under the McKinney Act is too low to deal with even the most urgent needs of the increasing numbers of homeless. In many cities, the number of homeless individuals and families whose requests for emergency shelter are turned down due to limited beds is increasing. Opening up more emergency shelters cannot be a solution, however. The focus of the funding under the act should be early prevention of homelessness among the vulnerable population groups and placing the homeless in permanent housing rather than in emergency shelters. The National Coalition for the Homeless believes that the act should have been authorized at a $2.5 billion level in 1998 in order to more realistically address the growth in homelessness (NCH, 1998b).

The 1990 Cranston–Gonzalez National Affordable Housing Act could also have been an important milestone. This act significantly revised the McKinney Act to make it more responsive to state and local situations. The core of the 1990 act is the Housing Opportunity Partnerships (HOP) program, which mandates states and localities to build a long-term investment partnership with the private sector and to develop a strategy to expand the supply of affordable housing with preference to rehabilitation of substandard stock. Another aspect of the act, HOPE (Home Ownership and Opportunities for People Everywhere) initiatives, would help low-income families buy public housing and other foreclosed property owned by HUD, provide supportive services to voucher recipients, provide rental assistance and supportive services for homeless persons with disabilities, and so on (U.S. Senate, 1990). Despite its good intention, however, the level of appropriation under the act has been far short of what is needed to increase low-income housing stocks, to prevent homelessness, and to help homeless families obtain permanent housing. Lack of federal dollars and initiatives also translates into lack of state-sponsored programs aimed at preventing homelessness. The curtailment of various social service budgets and the resulting budget shortfalls as well as a general lack of political will explain the lack of state programs for the prevention of homelessness (Johnson & Hambrick, 1993).

The federal homeless assistance policies have also been fraught with the inflexibility of its regulations governing the Emergency Assistance (EA) portion of the AFDC program. That is, funds from the EA program used to be restricted to housing families only in temporary shelters for a limited period. It was an irony that a family evicted for nonpayment of rent would then be housed in a shelter for over $3,000 a month, when the same amount could have kept them in their apartment for more than a year (Dugger, 1993; Messinger, 1993). With the 1996 welfare reform, each state is now responsible for setting eligibility criteria and benefit level for the TANF recipients. As the time limit on welfare receipt is implemented, those who are the most vulnerable, lacking any job skills, may not be able to make a successful transition from welfare to work and thus may be at risk of losing their ability to pay rent by losing eligibility for a welfare grant.

Shelters, Transitional Housing, and Welfare Hotels

The most notable program that appeared in response to the increase in the numbers of homeless families since the mid-1980s was the opening of a large number of family shelters. An up-to-date, accurate count of family shelters nationwide does not exist, with the most recent information dating back to 1988, the year that HUD conducted a nationwide probability survey of shelters. The survey estimated a few more than 5,000 (an increase from 1,900 in 1984) shelters, 39% of which were family shelters serving 20,000 to 30,000 family groups nightly. All family shelters are nonprofit, supported by a combination of public (HUD, FEMA, Community Development Block Grant [CDBG]), and other federal, state, and local sources and private funds.

The biggest source of financial support for emergency shelter is, of course, the McKinney Act; Title III authorizes and formally defines the emergency food and shelter program. It requires the FEMA director to establish a national board to administer the program and specifies as board members the director and representatives from six private organizations—the United Way, the Salvation Army, the National Council of Churches of Christ, Catholic Charities, the Council of Jewish Federation, and the American Red Cross. Localities designated by the national board create local boards, with the mayor or other head of local government replacing the FEMA director. The local boards determine which local government or private nonprofit entities receive funding to provide services under the program (Foscarinis, 1995). The money can be used to provide food, consumable supplies essential to the operation of shelters and mass-feeding facilities, per diem sheltering cost, small equipment, the limited leasing of capital equipment, utility and rent/mortgage assistance to people on the verge of becoming homeless, first month's rent to help families and individuals move out of shelters or other precarious circumstances and into stable environments, emergency lodging, and minor rehabilitation of shelter facilities (Foscarinis, 1995; Hombs, 1994). Emergency shelters, as indicated in the title, are usually temporary in terms of duration of individuals' or families' stay.

Subtitle B, Emergency Shelter Grants (ESG), of Title IV (which is administered by HUD) of the McKinney Act also offers funds to cities, counties, and states that have a comprehensive homeless assistance plan approved by HUD, according to a formula based on population and poverty and with a 50% matching requirement. Local governments receiving ESG may distribute those funds to private nonprofit organizations. Funds may be used for renovation or conversion of buildings for emergency shelters; provision of "essential services," including employment, health, drug abuse, or education; and maintenance and operation of shelter facilities (but not staff) (Foscarinis, 1995).

Subtitle C of Title IV provides funds for transitional housing facilities, which provide longer-term housing along with supportive services that prepare individuals and families to enter the conventional housing market and establish independent living "within a reasonable amount of

time." This transitional housing results from the view that many homeless families need training in budgeting and parenting skills as well as
rehabilitation from substance abuse if they are to avoid further episodes
of homelessness (Rossi, 1994).

Subtitle C also provides funds for community-based permanent housing for disabled homeless people with supportive services. Funds distributed under subtitles B and C may be used for the acquisition and/
or rehabilitation of buildings to supply supportive housing, for some
operating costs of such housing, and for technical assistance to establish and operate supportive housing projects (Foscarinis, 1995).

In large cities, so-called welfare hotels are also contracted out by
local social service departments to house homeless families for short
or long periods. Because there are virtually no supportive services in
these hotels except the families' occasional contact with social services
departments or agencies regarding permanent housing or other needs,
they have the atmosphere of warehouses for the homeless. Many welfare
hotels are also notorious for their dangerous and chaotic living environment, as drug-related violence frequently erupts in the hallways where
children, denied any other play space, often venture out (Kozol, 1988,
1995).

(Shelters are specifically designed for emergency food and shelter
needs, and most shelters limit the length of stay they allow. We cannot
deny that, though they are available for only short periods, shelters
help homeless families by providing a roof over the heads of thousands
who might otherwise be sleeping on the streets, which can be dangerous
as well as harmful to their health. For families with children who have
been evicted or have fled from domestic abuse and/or dangerous neighborhoods and who have no other place to go, shelters are a saving
grace, a place where they can sleep, eat, and take care of bodily hygiene.
Moreover, more than 85% of the family shelters provide some form of
counseling, and an even higher proportion offer housing and other
entitlement services through referrals to other agencies (Rossi, 1994;
Weinreb & Rossi, 1995). Thus, shelters can provide more than temporary
lodging and help families link to resources vital for restoration of
their independence.

As temporary shelters have become transformed into permanent insti-
tutions, however, many problems have been found. The first has to do
with the escalating numbers of the homeless. Although thousands of
temporary shelters are now in operation throughout the country, according to the 1996 U.S. Conference of Mayors' survey of 29 cities, 20% of
all requests for emergency shelter went unmet due to lack of resources
(Waxman & Hinderliter, 1996). New York and West Virginia are the only

states that have identified the right to shelter within their constitutions (Stoner, 1995). New York City was the first and used to be the only city to provide emergency shelter to the homeless on demand (with an allowable wait of two or more nights). But in 1996 it declared that all families who have been doubled up are automatically ineligible for shelter even when they and their hosts insist that they cannot return to the doubled-up situation.

The second problem also has to do with the increasing numbers of the homeless. As a result of the increasing requests, shelters tend to admit people beyond their optimal capacity, which in turn results in overcrowded, noisy, squalid, and often unsafe environments. Congregating in one place families that have severe economic and other related problems creates an environment that is detrimental to the proper physical, emotional, and cognitive development of children. In an effort to prevent potential chaos, keep order, and ensure efficient management with limited staff and/or volunteers, shelter administrations invariably adopt numerous rules and regulations to exert control over the physical and social environment of the shelter, and they are not often flexible in response to an individual's or a family's circumstances, to the detriment of the individual's or the family's welfare (Stark, 1994).

Third, as mentioned, shelters are not fundamental, or long-term, solutions to homelessness, because they do not add permanent housing units, improve conditions in cities, or prevent families from losing their home. The bottom line is that shelters do not address the causes of homelessness but are merely means of ameliorating the pain and suffering that follow loss of one's home. This mere Band-Aid treatment of homelessness may in fact divert money from housing construction and rehabilitation and from other social services and financial assistance for the poor (Ferlauto, 1991). The HUD reports published in 1994 and 1995 indicated that emergency shelter through the ESG cost the government $8,087 per bed annually, and the transitional/supportive housing demonstration program cost $10,695 per person annually. On the other hand, the average annual cost per unit of a Section 8 housing certificate was $5,280 in 1995, and even the most expensive short-term rental assistance program, specifically designed to prevent homelessness, cost less than half the Section 8 cost (National Law Center on Homelessness and Poverty, 1997; see also Johnson & Hambrick, 1993).

Fourth, shelter-based programs create unintended yet severe problems: Helping sheltered families tends to give them benefits that similarly situated poor families who do not enter or are denied space in a homeless shelter do not get (Berlin & McAllister, 1994). In a tight housing market, the housing service that sheltered families receive gives them a competitive edge over other poor families not served by a shelter. New York City's well-intentioned policy of awarding homeless families priority for permanent housing and accordingly moving them to public housing projects in a few months, bypassing nonhomeless families who had been on the waiting list for as long as 10 years, created an unantici-pated consequence: Housed families, seeking a shortcut to placement in public housing projects, soon began to declare themselves homeless (Stoner, 1995).

Last but not least, the flourishing of shelters hides these poor families from the public by warehousing them and may help foster the percep-tion that individual deficits rather than structural factors are responsi-ble for their homelessness. A comprehensive survey of public attitudes and beliefs about homeless people in 1990 found that Americans had mixed sentiments. An overwhelming majority considered homelessness a significant social problem requiring active housing programs from the federal government. Nonetheless, the respondents tended to associate the homeless population with other stigmatized groups, believing that the most important causes of homelessness are substance abuse and irresponsible behavior (Link et al., 1996). At the time of the survey, the country was in an economic recession. In 1998, when the country had a booming economy, the public seemed to be even more likely to blame the victims. The symptom management–oriented approach, which pro-vides food and shelter but often little else, is likely to be at once a result as well as a cause of the victim-blaming sentiments.

REFERENCES

Ames, D. L., Brown, N. C., Callahan, M. H., Cummings, S. B., Smock, S. M., & Ziegler, J. M. (1992). Rethinking American urban policy. *Journal of Urban Affairs, 14*(3/4), 197–216.

Bassuk, E. L. (1990). Who are the homeless families? Characteristics of sheltered mothers and children. *Community Mental Health Journal, 26*(5), 425–434.

Bassuk, E. L. (1992). Women and children without shelter: The characteristics of homeless families. In M. J. Robertson & M. Greenblatt (Eds.), *Homelessness: A national perspective* (pp. 257–264). New York: Plenum.

Bassuk, E. L., Browne, A., & Buckner, J. C. (1996, October). Single mothers and welfare. *Scientific American, 275*, 60–67.

Bassuk, E. L., Buckner, J. C., Weinreb, L. F., Browne, A., Bassuk, S. S., Dawson, R., & Perloff, J. N. (1997). Homelessness in female-headed families: Childhood and adult risk and protective factors. *American Journal of Public Health, 87*, 241–248.

Bassuk, E. L., & Gallagher, E. M. (1990). The impact of homelessness on children. In N. A. Boxill (Ed.), *Homeless children: The watchers and the waiters* (pp. 19–34). Binghamton, NY: The Haworth Press.

Bassuk, E. L., & Rosenberg, L. (1988). Why does family homelessness occur? A case control study. *American Journal of Public Health, 78*, 783–788.

———. (1990). Psychosocial characteristics of homeless children and children with homes. *Pediatrics, 85*(3), 257–261.

Bassuk, E. L., & Rubin, L. (1987). Homeless children: A neglected population. *American Journal of Orthopsychiatry, 57*(2), 279–286.

Bassuk, E. L., & Weinreb, L. (1994). The plight of homeless children. In J. Blacher (Ed.), *When there's no place like home* (pp. 37–62). Baltimore: Paul H. Brooks.

Baum, A. S., & Burnes, D. W. (1993). *A nation in denial: The truth about homelessness*. Boulder, CO: Westview.

Baumann, S. L. (1993). The meaning of being homeless. *Scholarly Inquiry for Nursing Practice: An International Journal, 7*(1), 59–70.

Berck, J. (1992, Spring). No place to be: Voices of homeless children. *Public Welfare*, 28–33.

Berlin, G., & McAllister, W. (1994). Homeless family shelters and family homelessness. *American Behavioral Scientist, 37*(3), 422–434.

Bernstein, A. B., Alperstein, G., & Fierman, A. H. (1988, November). *Health care of homeless children*. Paper presented at the meeting of the American Public Health Association, Chicago.

Blau, J. (1992). *The visible poor: Homelessness in the United States*. New York: Oxford University Press.

Boxill, N. A., & Beaty, A. L. (1990). Mother/child interaction among homeless women and their children in a public night shelter in Atlanta, Georgia. In N. A. Boxill (Ed.), *Homeless children: The watchers and the waiters* (pp. 49–64). Binghamton, NY: The Haworth Press.

Brooks, M. G., & Buckner, J. C. (1996). Work and welfare: Job histories, barriers to employment, and predictors to work among low-income single mothers. *American Journal of Orthopsychiatry, 66*, 525–537.

Browne, A. (1993). Family violence and homelessness: The relevance of trauma histories in the lives of homeless women. *American Journal of Orthopsychiatry, 63*(3), 370–383.

Burg, M. A. (1994). Health problems of sheltered homeless women and their dependent children. *Health and Social Work, 19*(2), 125–131.

Burt, M. R., & Cohen, B. E. (1989). Differences among homeless single women, women with children, and single men. *Social Problems, 36*, 508–524.

Butler, S. S. (1994). *Middle-aged, female and homeless: The stories of a forgotten group*. New York: Garland.

Concord Coalition. (1997). *Average income received by each fifth of households: 1967–1995* [on line]. Available: people.delphi.com/rd100/income.html.

daCosta Nunez, R. (1994). *Hopes, dreams, and promise: The future of homeless children in America*. New York: Homes for the Homeless.

DeAngelis, T. (1994). Homeless families: Stark reality of the '90s. *American Psychological Association Monitor, 25*(4), 1–39.

DiBiase, R., & Waddell, S. (1995). Some effects of homelessness on the psychological functioning of preschoolers. *Journal of Abnormal Child Psychology*, *23*, 783–792.

Dolbeare, C. N. (1996). Housing policy: A general consideration. In J. Baumohl (Ed.), *Homelessness in America* (pp. 34–45). Phoenix: Oryx.

Donahue, P. J., & Tuber, S. B. (1995). The impact of homelessness on children's level of aspiration. *Bulletin of the Menninger Clinic*, *59*, 249–255.

Dornbusch, S. M. (1993). Some political implications of the Stanford studies of homeless families. In S. Matteo (Ed.), *American women in the nineties* (pp. 153–172). Boston: Northeastern University Press.

Dugger, C. W. (1993, July 26). Homeless shelters drain money from housing, experts say. *New York Times*, p. B1.

Dupper, D. R., & Halter, A. P. (1994). Barriers in educating children from homeless shelters: Perspectives of school and shelter staff. *Social Work in Education*, *16*(1), 39–45.

Fainstein, S. S., & Fainstein, N. (1995). A proposal for urban policy in the 1990s. *Urban Affairs Review*, *30*, 630–634.

Ferlauto, R. C. (1991, Summer). A new approach to low-income housing. *Public Welfare*, 30–35.

Foscarinis, M. (1995, November–December). Shelter and housing: Programs under the Stewart B. McKinney Homeless Assistance Act. *Clearinghouse Review*, *29*, 760–770.

———. (1996). The federal response: The Stewart B. McKinney Homeless Assistance Act. In J. Baumohl (Ed.), *Homelessness in America* (pp. 160–171). Phoenix: Oryx.

Goodman, L. A. (1991). The prevalence of abuse among homeless and housed poor mothers: A comparison study. *American Journal of Orthopsychiatry*, *61*, 489–500.

Hagen, J. L. (1987). Gender and homelessness. *Social Work*, *32*, 312–316.

Hausman, B., & Hammen, C. (1993). Parenting in homeless families: The double crisis. *American Journal of Orthopsychiatry*, *63*, 358–369.

Hombs, M. E. (1994). *American homelessness: A reference handbook* (2nd ed.). Santa Barbara, CA: ABC-CLIO.

Jencks, C. (1994). *The homeless*. Cambridge, MA: Harvard University Press.

Johnson, A. K., & Cnaan, R. A. (1995). Social work practice with homeless persons: State of the art. *Research on Social Work Practice*, *5*(3), 340–382.

Johnson, A. K., & Kreuger, L. W. (1989, November). Toward a better understanding of homeless women. *Social Work*, *34*, 537–540.

Johnson, A. K., McChesney, K. Y., Rocha, C. J., & Butterfield, W. H. (1995). Demographic differences between sheltered homeless families and housed poor families: Implications for policy and practice. *Journal of Sociology and Social Welfare*, *22*(4), 5–22.

Johnson, G. T., & Hambrick, R. S. (1993). Preventing homelessness: Virginia's homeless intervention program. *Journal of Urban Affairs*, *15*(6), 473–489.

Joint Center for Housing Studies. (1995). *The state of the nation's housing 1995*. Cambridge, MA: Harvard University.

————. (1996). *The state of the nation's housing 1996*. Cambridge, MA: Harvard University.

————. (1997). *The state of the nation's housing 1997*. Cambridge, MA: Harvard University.

Joint Economic Committee. (1992). *Teenage pregnancy: The economic and social cost*. Hearing before the Subcommittee on Education and Health of the 102nd Congress of the United States. Washington, DC: U.S. Government Printing Office.

Kasarda, J. D. (1989). Urban industrial transition and the underclass. *Annals of the American Academy of Political and Social Sciences, 501,* 26–47.

Khanna, M., Singh, N. N., Nemil, M., Best, A., & Ellis, C. R. (1992). Homeless women and their families: Characteristics, life circumstances, and needs. *Journal of Child and Family Studies, 1*(2), 155–165.

Kilpatrick, K. L., Litt, M., & Williams, L. M. (1997). Post-traumatic stress disorder in child witnesses to domestic violence. *American Journal of Orthopsychiatry, 67,* 639–644.

Koegel, P., Burnam, M. A., & Baumohl, J. (1996). The causes of homelessness. In J. Baumohl (Ed.), *Homelessness in America* (pp. 24–33). Phoenix: Oryx.

Kondratas, A. (1991). Ending homelessness: Policy challenges. *American Psychologist, 46*(1), 1226–1231.

Kozol, J. (1988). *Rachel and her children: Homeless families in America*. New York: Crown.

————. (1995). *Amazing grace*. New York: Crown.

Leonard, P. A., Dolbeare, C. N., & Lazere, E. B. (1989). *A place to call home: The crisis in housing for the poor*. Washington, DC: Center on Budget and Policy Priorities and Low Income Housing Information Service.

Liebow, E. (1993). *Tell them who I am: The lives of homeless women*. New York: Basic Books.

Link, B., Phelan, J., Bresnahan, M., Stueve, A., Moore, R., & Susser, E. (1995). Lifetime and five-year prevalence of homelessness in the United States: New evidence on an old debate. *American Journal of Orthopsychiatry, 65,* 347–354.

Link, B., Phelan, J., Stueve, A., Moore, R., Bresnahan, M., & Struening, E. (1996). Public attitudes and beliefs about homeless people. In J. Baumohl (Ed.), *Homelessness in America* (pp. 143–148). Phoenix: Oryx.

Link, B., Susser, E., Stueve, A., Phelan, J., Moore, R., & Struening, E. (1994). Lifetime and five-year prevalence of homelessness in the United States. *American Journal of Public Health, 84,* 1907–1912.

Lipsky, M., & Smith, S. R. (1989, March). When social problems are treated as emergencies. *Social Service Review, 63,* 5–25.

Marcuse, P. (1996). Space and race in the post-Fordist city: The outcast ghetto and advanced homelessness in the United States today. In E. Mingione (Ed.), *Urban poverty and the underclass* (pp. 176–217). Cambridge, MA: Blackwell.

Massey, D. S. (1994, December). America's apartheid and the urban underclass. *Social Service Review, 68,* 471–487.

Massey, D. S., Gross, A. B., & Shibuya, K. (1994, June). Migration, segregation, and the geographic concentration of poverty. *American Sociological Review, 59,* 425–445.

Masten, A. S. (1992). Homeless children in the United States: Mark of a nation at risk. *Current Directions in Psychological Science, 1,* 42–44.

Masten, A. S., Sesma, A., Si-Asar, R., Lawrence, C., Miliotis, D., & Dionne, J. A. (1997). Educational risks for children experiencing homelessness. *Journal of School Psychology, 35*(1), 27–46.

McChesney, K. Y. (1990). Family homelessness: A systemic problem. *Journal of Social Issues, 46*(4), 191–205.

———. (1992). Homeless families: Four patterns of poverty. In M. J. Robertson & M. Greenblatt (Eds.), *Homelessness: A national perspective* (pp. 245–256). New York: Plenum.

———. (1993). Homeless families since 1990: Implications for education. *Education and Urban Society, 25,* 361–380.

———. (1995, September). A review of the empirical literature on contemporary urban homeless families. *Social Service Review, 69,* 429–460.

McNamee, M. J., Bartek, J. J., & Lynes, D. (1994). Health problems of sheltered homeless children using mobile health services. *Issues in Comprehensive Pediatric Nursing, 17,* 233–242.

Messinger, R. W. (1993, August 7). Out of hotels, into homes. *New York Times.*

Mihaly, L. (1991). Beyond numbers: Homeless families with children. In J. H. Kryder-Coe, L. M. Salamon, & J. M. Molnar (Eds.), *Homeless children and youth: A new American dilemma* (pp. 11–32). New Brunswick, NJ: Transaction.

National Coalition for the Homeless. (1998a). *NCH fact sheet* [on line]. Available: nch.ari.net/html.

———. (1998b). *Position paper on HUD McKinney Reauthorization* [on line]. Available: nch.ari.net/hr/217.html.

National Law Center on Homelessness and Poverty. (1997). *Housing options* [on line]. Available: www.nlchp.org/housing.html.

National Low Income Housing Coalition. (1997). *Critical issues pending in public and assisted housing reform legislation: H.R. 2 and S. 462* [on line]. Available: www.nlihc.org/pubhsg.html.

———. (1998). *Fair market rent and poverty* [on line]. Available: www.nlihc. org/oor3.html.

Passaro, J. (1996). *The unequal homeless: Men on the streets, women in their place.* New York: Routledge.

Rafferty, Y. (1995). The legal rights and educational problems of homeless children and youth. *Educational Evaluation and Policy Analysis, 17*(1), 39–61.

Rafferty, Y., & Shinn, M. (1991). The impact of homelessness on children. *American Psychologist, 46*(11), 1170–1179.

Rank, M. R. (1994). *Living on the edge: The realities of welfare in America.* New York: Columbia University Press.

Rescorla, L., Parker, R., & Stolley, P. (1991). Ability, achievement, and adjustment in homeless children. *American Journal of Orthopsychiatry, 61*(2), 210–220.

Ringheim, K. (1993). Investigating the structural determinants of homelessness: The case of Houston. *Urban Affairs Quarterly, 28*(4), 617–640.

Rosenthal, R. (1994). *Homeless in paradise: A map of the terrain.* Philadelphia: Temple University Press.

Rossi, P. H. (1989). *Down and out in America: The origins of homelessness.* Chicago: University of Chicago Press.

———. (1994). Troubling families: Family homelessness in America. *American Behavioral Scientist, 37*(3), 342–395.

Salomon, A., Bassuk, S. S., & Brooks, M. G. (1996). Patterns of welfare use among poor and homeless women. *American Journal of Orthopsychiatry, 66*, 510–524.

Shane, P. G. (1996). *What about America's homeless children?* Thousand Oaks, CA: Sage.

Shinn, M., & Gillespie, C. (1994). The roles of housing and poverty in the origins of homelessness. *American Behavioral Scientist, 37*, 505–521.

Shinn, M., Knickman, J. R., & Weitzman, B. C. (1991). Social relationships and vulnerability to becoming homeless among poor families. *American Psychologist, 46*, 1180–1187.

Shinn, M., & Weitzman, B. C. (1996). Homeless families are different. In J. Baumohl (Ed.), *Homelessness in America* (pp. 109–122). Phoenix: Oryx.

Snow, D. A., Anderson, L., & Koegel, P. (1994). Distorting tendencies in research on the homeless. *American Behavioral Scientist, 37*(4), 461–475.

Stark, L. R. (1994). The shelter as "total institution": An organizational barrier to remedying homelessness. *American Behavioral Scientist, 37*, 553–562.

Steinbock, M. R. (1995). Homeless female-headed families: Relationships at risk. In S. M. H. Hanson et al. (Eds.), *Single parent families: Diversity, myths and realities* (pp. 143–159). Binghamton, NY: The Haworth Press.

Stoner, M. R. (1995). *The civil rights of homeless people: Law, social policy, and social work practice.* Hawthorne, NY: Aldine De Gruyter.

Stretch, J., & Kreuger, L. W. (1992). Five-year cohort study of homeless families: A joint policy research venture. *Journal of Sociology and Social Welfare, 19*(4), 73–88.

Timmer, D. A., Eitzen, D. S., & Talley, K. D. (1994). *Paths to homelessness: Extreme poverty and the urban housing crisis.* Boulder, CO: Westview.

U.S. Bureau of the Census. (1995). *Income, poverty, and valuation of noncash benefits: 1993* (Current Population Reports, Series P60–188). Washington, DC: U.S. Government Printing Office.

———. (1997). *Poverty in the United States: 1996* (Current Population Reports: Consumer income, P60–198). Washington, DC: U.S. Government Printing Office.

U.S. Conference of Mayors. (1990). *A status report on hunger and homelessness in America's cities: 1990.* Washington, DC: Author.

U.S. Department of Housing and Urban Development. (1994). *Priority: Home!: The federal plan to break the cycle of homelessness.* Washington, DC: Author.

U.S. House of Representatives. (1990). *Public housing and Section 8 programs.* Hearing before the Subcommittee on Housing and Community Development of the Committee on Banking, Finance and Urban Affairs (Serial No. 101–91). Washington, DC: U.S. Government Printing Office.

———. (1993). *Need for permanent housing for the homeless.* Hearing before the Subcommittee on Housing and Community Development of the Committee on Banking, Finance and Urban Affairs (Serial No. 103–21). Washington, DC: U.S. Government Printing Office.

U.S. Senate. (1990). *Cranston-Gonzalez National Affordable Housing Act* (P.L. 101–625) (Senate Report No. 101–316). Washington, DC: U.S. Government Printing Office.

Vissing, Y. (1996). *Out of sight, out of mind: Homeless children and families in small town America.* Lexington: University Press of Kentucky.

Wacquant, L. J. D., & Wilson, W. J. (1989). The cost of racial and class exclusion in the inner city. *Annals of the American Academy of Political and Social Sciences, 501,* 8–25.

Wagner, J., & Menke, E. (1991). The depression of homeless children: A focus for nursing intervention. *Issues in Comprehensive Pediatric Nursing, 14,* 17–29.

Watson, V. (1996). Responses by the states to homelessness. In J. Baumohl (Ed.), *Homelessness in America* (pp. 172–178). Phoenix: Oryx.

Waxman, L., & Hinderliter, S. (1996). *A status report on hunger and homelessness in America's cities: 1996.* Washington, DC: U.S. Conference of Mayors.

Weinreb, L., & Rossi, P. H. (1995, March). The American homeless family shelter "system." *Social Service Review, 69,* 86–107.

Weitzman, B. C. (1989). Pregnancy and childbirth: Risk factors for homelessness. *Family Planning Perspectives, 21,* 175–178.

Weitzman, B. C., & Berry, C. (1994, June). *Formerly homeless families and the transition to permanent housing: High risk families and the role of intensive case management services.* Final report to the Edna McConnell Clark Foundation. New York: Health Research Program, Robert F. Wagner Graduate School, New York University.

Weitzman, B. C., Knickman, J. R., & Shinn, M. (1990). Pathways to homelessness among New York City families. *Journal of Social Issues, 46*(4), 125–140.

———. (1992). Predictors of shelter use among low-income families: Psychiatric history, substance abuse, and victimization. *American Journal of Public Health, 82*(11), 1547–1550.

Whitman, B. Y., Accardo, P., Boyert, M., & Kendagor, R. (1990). Homelessness and cognitive performance in children: A possible link. *Social Work, 35*(6), 516–519.

Wilson, W. J. (1987). *The truly disadvantaged.* Chicago: University of Chicago Press.

———. (1996). *When work disappears: The world of the new urban poor.* New York: Vintage Books.

Wood, D., Valdez, R. B., Hayashi, T., & Shen, A. (1990). Homeless and housed families in Los Angeles: A study comparing demographic, economic, and family function characteristics. *American Journal of Public Health, 80,* 1049–1052.

Wright, J. D. (1990). Homeless is not healthy for children and other living things. In N. A. Boxill (Ed.), *Homeless children: The watchers and the waiters* (pp. 65–88). Binghamton, NY: The Haworth Press.

———. (1991). Poverty, homelessness, health, nutrition, and children. In J. H. Kryder-Coe, L. M. Salamon, & J. M. Molnar (Eds.), *Homeless children and youth: A new American dilemma* (pp. 71–103). New Brunswick, NJ: Transaction.

Ziesemer, C., Marcoux, L., & Marwell, B. E. (1994). Homeless children: Are they different from other low-income children? *Social Work*, *39*(6), 658–668.

Zima, B. T., Wells, K. B., & Freeman, H. E. (1994). Emotional and behavioral problems and severe academic delays among sheltered homeless children in Los Angeles County. *American Journal of Public Health*, *84*, 260–264.

Zorza, J. (1991). Woman battering: A major cause of homelessness. *Clearinghouse Review*, 421–429.

2

Research Methods

In the summer of 1994 we received a small research grant from the Baldy Center for Law and Social Policy of the State University of New York at Buffalo to start interviewing 20 families staying at two local shelters as part of our qualitative study of homeless parents and their children. The purpose of the interviews was to discover the homeless parents' own perception of the circumstances under which they became homeless and the effect of homelessness on their children's well-being.

The decision to focus on subjective experiences of the homeless parents derived from the primary author's frustration with existing research on homeless families with children. While teaching homelessness in her social policy course for graduate social work students, she found that most studies of homeless families, with the exception of Jonathan Kozol's *Rachel and Her Children* (1988), were based on description and analysis of demographic characteristics and/or other quantitative measures such as depressive symptoms of both parents and children, academic performance of children, and the likelihood of the families' exit from homelessness. These quantitative studies have been much needed to increase our understanding of the etiology and epidemiology of homelessness, and they are believed to have made significant contributions to shaping social policy and social services for the homeless.

Considering that homelessness must be one of the most (if not the most) trying circumstances in the family's life, however, we thought it important to find out what homeless families perceive of their homelessness and how they cope during this trying time. After all, these families are the ones who go through homelessness and thus have the most intimate perception and knowledge of what the experience entails. They are the ones who should be providing the most valuable input to policy makers and social service providers. The primary focus of our study needed to be on homeless parents who struggle to maintain family cohesiveness and to raise their children in the midst of the myriad of crisis situations. Another important focus of the study needed to be on children, who are clearly the least fortunate victims of poverty and homelessness. Because many children were too young to articulate their emotional status, we decided to ask parents about what their children were going through.

In other words, we felt that we needed to obtain valid and reliable data about family homelessness and to understand and critically analyze this most serious social problem from an inside-out, not outside-in perspective. Considering the painful nature and effect of homelessness, we also felt that understanding and critical analysis of homelessness needed to be anchored in our sensitivity to the suffering of the homeless. To achieve these goals, we decided to conduct a qualitative study. The question How do homeless families perceive and manage their homelessness? was too broad and unstructured for a quantitative investigation. We also believed that a qualitative study was better suited to formulating and presenting a coherent theory that needed to be constructed ground up, chiefly from homeless parents' own stories relating their pain and suffering, without interference from researchers' biases and/or assumptions.

We were aware that our biases and/or assumptions were partly attributable to prevailing theories or ideas about homelessness, which have so far been constructed primarily from the interpretation of quantitative data. To minimize the possibly negative effects that our biases/assumptions might have on the study, we thought it important to be aware of such biases/assumptions. Nevertheless, we had no intention of discrediting the sources of them, that is, existing theories and ideas; instead, we presented them in the preceding chapter "as a backdrop to sensitize and illuminate the data or to enlighten the researcher" (Morse, 1994, p. 29).

In an effort to understand the problems, needs, and coping strategies of homeless families from the families' perspectives, we interviewed the first 20 parents who stayed in two shelters in the summer of 1994. We asked each participating parent a series of open-ended questions regarding the reasons for their homelessness, covering their economic and housing circumstances before they entered the shelter (including doubled-up living arrangements), and their concerns about their children, including changes in the children's emotional, behavioral, physical, and educational statuses. Each interview took 1 to 3 hours. We hoped to find certain patterns or similarities as well as differences among them with respect to their perceptions of problems, needs, and coping strategies.

When we analyzed the transcripts of those 20 interviews, we realized that the parents were telling us a lot more than we had asked for. For example, the questions regarding their circumstances before they entered the shelter led many parents to talk about their social support networks/systems. Most notably, we found that they had strong feelings about shelter rules, hygiene, and treatment by the staff. Because these parents were interviewed at shelters, they naturally talked a lot about their experiences of shelter life, which were very much affected by the physical, structural, and personnel conditions of the shelters. We also realized that the parents were extremely frustrated with the process and prospects/outcomes of their search for decent housing. As a result of the analysis of this first round of interviews, we decided to add questions to generate additional data regarding social support systems, shelter living, and barriers to finding decent housing for the next 60 interviews, which we conducted in late 1995 through June 1997 and for which we subsequently obtained additional funding from the Baldy Center.

Our qualitative research methodology may be summarized as a blending of phenomenology and the grounded theory. This type of blending may indeed be in danger of "method slurring" or "muddling methods" and may violate the rigor that each approach requires to maintain the consistency of its underlying assumptions (Baker, Wuest, & Stern, 1992; Stern, 1994). Given the nature of homelessness as an intensely personal experience as well as a serious social problem that occurs within the context of a specific society, however, we were compelled to engage in method slurring. According to Baker et al. (1992), the goal of empirical phenomenological research is to "describe the world-as-experienced by the participants of the inquiry in order to discover the common meanings underlying empirical variations of a given phenomenon" (p. 1356). The researcher must identify and suspend what he or she already knows about the experience and approach the phenomenon without preconceptions. In grounded theory, which is rooted in the symbolic interactionist school of sociology, the researcher needs to understand behavior as the participants understand it, to learn about their world, to learn their interpretation of self in the interaction, and to share their definitions (Chenitz & Swanson, 1986). Thus, the grounded theory "aims to generate theoretical constructs which explain the 'action' or 'what is going on here' in a social context," with the final goal of generating inductively based theoretical explanations of social and psychological processes (Habermann-Little, 1991, p. 189; see also Baker et al., 1992; Stern, 1980; Strauss & Corbin, 1990). We intended that, through our analysis of data, not only would we discover the common/personal meanings of homelessness, but also we would contribute to expanding the existing theory base.

SAMPLE AND INTERVIEW METHODS

With the plan of a qualitative study of homeless parents, we first contacted the Erie County Commission on Homelessness, an organization of shelter administrators, social service agency representatives, and concerned citizens, in the spring of 1994 to obtain an approval for the study. The commission enthusiastically supported the study plan and provided the list of all family shelters in the city of Buffalo and the vicinity. We eliminated shelters that served certain population groups only—the developmentally disabled, the mentally ill, and domestic violence victims—and selected two that did not have any eligibility restrictions. We chose a third shelter in Syracuse by directly contacting its director. It was chosen also because one of the interviewers was familiar with the environment through her previous work. We went out to those three shelters to explain the purpose of the study to the staff and subsequently obtained permission to conduct the study from their boards of directors and/or other decision-making bodies. We obtained approval from the SUNY at Buffalo's Committee on Human Subjects.

The Erie County Commission on Homelessness told us that, based on reports from area shelters, more than 500 families with children were homeless in Buffalo in 1994. This number is believed to be an underestimate, because not all homeless families enter shelters and not all shelters provided relevant information. An accurate count of homeless families with children in Syracuse was not available either. Buffalo, in western New York, is the second-largest city in the state, after New York City, and Syracuse, in upstate New York, is the third-largest city. In terms of the average fair market rental in 1996, those in Buffalo ($424 for one bedroom and $510 for two bedrooms) and Syracuse ($448 for one bedroom and $554 for two bedrooms) fall in the nation's median ranges ($449 for one bedroom and $558 for two bedrooms) (National Low Income Housing Coalition, 1997). Like other big cities across the country, both Buffalo and Syracuse have racially segregated inner-city neighborhoods where poverty and crime rates far exceed those of other neighborhoods. Especially in Buffalo, an old city that saw its glory in the 1880s, the inner-city neighborhoods are crowded with old, dilapidated housing stocks inhabited mostly by the poor.

Selection of interviewees was arranged by the staff, who announced the study to the residents of the shelter and recruited volunteer potential study participants. We asked the staff to post on the shelter bulletin board the flyers that we had prepared to describe the study and solicit interviewees. Of the volunteers recruited, we selected only those who had stayed more than a week at the shelter by the time of the interview. For the purpose of collecting accurate information on children's academic issues, interviews, with the exception of the first 20, were conducted only during the school year. All three shelters provided a quiet space for the interviews. At the beginning of the interview, each participating parent was provided with a letter of informed consent in which it was explained that the interview would be taped and later transcribed and that he or she was free to withdraw at any time if he or she so wished without losing the $25 offered as compensation for his or her time. No one withdrew before the completion of the interview, which lasted for 1 to 3 1/2 hours. It appeared that most parents were initially attracted to the interview by the $25 fee, given that it was a significant sum for the poorest. However, an overwhelming majority of the participating parents also appeared to genuinely welcome the opportunity to tell their side of the story to a sympathetic listener. As suggested by other interviewer-researchers of the homeless and the housed poor (Dash, 1996; Rosenthal, 1994), the disenfranchised are often glad to have the chance to be listened to because they are aware that their voices have seldom been heard. We believe that our emphasis on the confidential nature of the interview as well as our objective stance and the absence of any tie between the shelters and our research project also assured the parents that we would not pose any threat to their shelter stay or at least do no further harm to their situation.

All 80 interviews were done by four social workers, including the second author of the book, who had had extensive experience in working with disadvantaged families with children. Before they set out to interview the parents, the interviewers were trained by the authors in the ways of conducting qualitative interviews. Each interview started with the parent's filling out or answering a brief questionnaire on demographic data—age, level of education, marital status, number of children, and so on. The interviewer then started the qualitative part of the interview. The interviewers were trained to take the role of sympathetic listeners and to encourage the parents to present their feelings/views/opinions in a spontaneous and meaningful way, using the interview schedule as a guide to assist the spontaneous flow of the account but to anchor it within the boundaries of the research questions. At the end of the interview, each parent was also asked to fill out or verbally answer the Eyberg Child Behavior Inventory for each of his or her children between the ages of 2 and 16. The interviewers provided periodic input to and shared tips with one another with respect to interviewing skills to maintain consistency in the data collection phase. The second author interviewed 50 families, and the other three social workers each interviewed 10 families (including 10 families in Syracuse). Each interviewer transcribed her interviews verbatim, with the exception of the names and any other identifying information on the interviewees and their families, and the transcript was reviewed by both the interviewers and the authors. All of the names were replaced by randomly chosen aliases, and the other identifying information was also altered to disguise the interviewees' true identities. Each interviewer was able to interview one to four parents at each visit, and they provided us their observations of the physical environment of the shelter and their impressions of the shelter atmosphere.

METHODS OF ANALYSIS

The basic cognitive processes of data analysis we engaged in consisted of comprehending, synthesizing, theorizing, and recontextualizing (Morse, 1994). For a basic frame of reference for data analysis as well as a guide to specific and concrete methods of qualitative analysis, we relied on suggestions from many sources (Habermann-Little, 1991; Keddy, Sims, & Stern, 1996; Leininger, 1994; Sandelowski, 1995; Stern, 1980; Strauss & Corbin, 1990). We also tailored certain methods of analysis to the specific nature of our raw data as we proceeded, as will be described later.

Comprehending

As a first step of data analysis, we read the interview transcripts, trying to familiarize ourselves with the content. Second, we reread them and did line-by-line, sentence, and paragraph analysis of the content, trying to identify concepts and to comprehend their meaning. We underlined important concepts and made notes of possible categories from what appeared to have been mentioned repetitively by a number of parents as well as from what appeared to be idiosyncratic to only one or a few parents. Third, as we became more sensitized to and enlightened about the data and their meaning in the process of our analysis, we went back to earlier transcripts several times and reanalyzed them according to our continuously evolving frame of analysis and expanded or realigned categories and codes, making data analysis a circular and evolving process. Fourth, throughout the process of data analysis, we engaged in discussion about the meanings and categories presented by the data and complemented each other's analytic efforts. Most of the time, we would work independently, then would together review and discuss the outcomes of the independent work to arrive at mutually agreed upon coding categories and interpretations. In the process of our analysis, we also presented parts of the data, our coded categories, and interpretations to a group of qualitative researchers, composed of PhD students and faculty in nursing, education, social work, women's studies, and history, as a check on reliability, and we received valuable feedback from these research colleagues.

We would like to highlight the fact that, as illustrated earlier, our data collection and analysis occurred concurrently. Each interview was transcribed and analyzed in the manner described in the preceding paragraph as soon as the interview was completed and was compared with the findings of the other interview transcripts. The insights gained from this preliminary analysis were fed back to the data collection process. Some questions (such as those on social support and children's health status) were modified, and others (such as questions regarding level of education and barriers to finding decent housing) were added to the next round of interviews. Throughout the progress of our study, we used this simultaneous and iterative data collection and analysis process, rather than a fixed, linear process. The reliability and validity of our study has been enhanced by this constantly emergent and reflective approach.

Because of the sheer volume of the raw data, however, we felt from the beginning of our data analysis the need for a mechanism that would provide some structure to allow us to see these categories, notes, and other coding devices as a whole for all participants. We felt that such a mechanism would enable us to easily discover vertical, or interfamily, as well as horizontal, or intrafamily, connections, comparisons, and complementation among and within these categories. The next step in qualitative analysis, the synthesizing process, required us to be able to sift through and aggregate stories and build composite descriptions (Morse, 1994). To create some type of visual presentation of a summary appeared to be a logical necessity for us to be able engage in that next step.

We examined the possibility of using computer-based software to analyze the qualitative data for this purpose, but we decided against using such a program simply because the available programs functioned more like index cards that would need to be shuffled through rather than like a spreadsheet that would show all the data on the same surface. In fact, the model for our ideal visual matrix was a spreadsheet program. We constructed eight sheets of 26-by-14-inch poster board, with about 40 vertical lines and 25 columns of varying width. Each sheet could contain information on 10 families, and each family was separated by a clear vertical line of color. In the left-hand side columns, we transferred basic demographic data: an assigned family number (1 through 80); parents' age(s), race, level of education, and marital status; number and ages of all children born to the parent(s); number and ages of the parents' children staying at the shelter; relationship to current caretakers of children not staying at the shelter; number of times the family had moved in the preceding 24 months; types of children's physical and psychosocial problems; and Eyberg Scale scores for the children. These demographic and other quantifiable variables were later copied to the data window of the *SPSS for Windows* for a statistical analysis, the results of which results were later presented in Tables 2.1 through 2.4.

In much wider columns, we also transferred qualitative data, corresponding to each family, under such column headings as reasons for losing home, neighborhoods, times previously homeless and reasons, living arrangement before entering the shelter, work status, income before the shelter and now, social support, children's physical problems, children's psychosocial and adjustment problems, children's academic problems, prenatal and birth-related problems, wishes, shelter experiences, and barriers to finding decent housing. These column headings represented the research questions we asked the interviewee parents. In addition to these headings, we had an "other" column at the right-hand side of the poster. This column was a wide-open space reserved for content that would not fall under any other column heading. In each column, in addition to making notes about concepts and categories that were the results of the line-by-line, sentence, and paragraph analyses, we transferred parts of the quotations (and the page numbers of the transcript) that we would like to go back to for details in the synthesizing process.

In order to prime readers to the characteristics of our sample families, we also quantified some of the qualitative data and did frequency tabulations. We thought that readers would like to be aware of the extent, as well as the nature and depth, of problems leading to family homelessness and the effects of homelessness on the families. For example, they may wonder about the proportion of families who became homeless due primarily to nonpayment of rent versus the proportion of those who became homeless due primarily to domestic violence. We believe that the quantified information complements the qualitative information.

Synthesizing

The completed posters allowed us to compare different families vertically and, at the same time, to examine the whole range of data pertaining to each family horizontally. Thus, it served as a visual summary of the raw data as well as a handy reference to the actual content of the transcripts. Aided by this visual summary, we started to synthesize the information. First, through inter- and intrafamily comparing and complementing, we reviewed and reexamined the categories that we had teased out or constructed from our earlier content analysis. Specifically, we grouped and sorted out commonalities, or repeated patterns, as well as heterogeneities, or idiosyncratic themes, in those categories and tried to establish a meaningful system of codes by merging, separating, and relabeling them. We would like to point out that this reconfiguring process was guided by both inductive and deductive logic: inductive, by looking at the data; deductive, by referring to existing literature that we reviewed in the preceding chapter. Second, using these codes as retrieval and organizing devices, we made clusters of related segments of the interviews by cutting and pasting all relevant parts of the transcripts. Third, we eliminated redundant or superfluous quotations in an effort to construct and present the stories in an aggregate and substantive yet concise manner.

The fourth step in synthesizing was to weave the stories that emerged in each category into a composite description. In fact, weaving stories was one of the easier processes because many categories were already interconnected, and trying to separate them out had proved to be a rather difficult job. For example, substance abuse and domestic violence were coexisting reasons for homelessness for some families. We also found interconnectedness among certain columns in the poster. For example, the reasons for losing one's home and the neighborhood where the families used to live, doubled-up living arrangements and social support system, and the organizational flexibility of a shelter and the family's shelter experience were three linked pairs, and thus the stories would be coherent only when all the elements were put together.

The most important of all, if not the least unexpected, link was the inherent interconnectedness in the families' economic and housing circumstances before they lost their home; their reasons for homelessness; their children's physical, psychosocial, and academic problems; their shelter experiences; and the prospects for their future economic and housing situations. This whole picture, which contain these families' past, present, and future prospects, was needed to understand the problems of homelessness.

The fifth and most important step in synthesizing was to bring forward the feelings/views/assessments of the parents themselves within this picture, so as to really answer our research question How do homeless families perceive and manage homelessness? That is, the focus is on the families, whose pain, suffering, weaknesses, strengths, and resiliency under the circumstances need to be the key to understanding the problems of homelessness. However, the synthesis and crystallization of the families' perception was also a beginning step toward theorizing.

Theorizing and Recontextualizing

The ultimate purpose of this study was to present policy makers and social service providers with an enriched understanding of the social problems of homelessness from the perspective of homeless families. The building blocks of this enriched understanding consisted of the composite descriptions of stories relating to the families' pains and coping strategies. We also added interpretations of the themes found in the composite descriptions in order to facilitate our understanding of the families' experience of homelessness. In our theorizing process, we tried to weld together these building blocks, our interpretations, and the existing knowledge base on homelessness into a structure that contains an alternative explanation of the etiology of homelessness among families; we also tried to provide further enlightenment on homeless children's problems, the families' suffering and coping strategies, and the temporary shelter systems. We use the word *alternative* because the structure that comes out of such a construction process may be different from the existing body of knowledge since the whole process has been anchored in the perspective of the homeless themselves. The structure, however, is not supposed to be a completed masterpiece but a work in progress that will need to be expanded, enhanced, and remodeled here and there in the future, as more knowledge that can form building blocks accumulates.

Our building-theory process was also one in which we tried to emphasize both the commonalities and the heterogeneities in experiences and perceptions of the families. In spite of some notable variances, however, the recurring patterns that emerged from the data generally support the relationships among urban deterioration, poverty, and homelessness. The findings also add to the existing knowledge base the debilitating effects of homelessness on both parents and children, who have already been swamped with problems engendered by chronic poverty, their helplessness, and the inadequacy of temporary shelter systems. We hope that understanding the realities of the added forces of victimization that homelessness brings upon the daily lives of poor families, especially children will serve as a spur to more concerted, systematic, and compassionate policies and programs to prevent homelessness.

CHARACTERISTICS OF SAMPLE FAMILIES

Of the 80 families we interviewed, 64 were headed by women who indicated that they were either unmarried (never married, divorced, or widowed) or separated (mostly victims of domestic violence and disputes or desertion by a husband); 3 families were headed by single fathers; 4 families were headed by married women whose husbands were not with them in the shelter because they were either in jail, in another state looking for work, or staying with a relative or a friend; and 9 families had both spouses/partners in the shelter. As shown in the data in Table 1, 70% of the parents were African-American, 24% were white, and 6% were Hispanic. The ages of the parents (mothers in the case of couples) ranged from 17 to 49, with mean and median being 30 and 31 years, respectively, and their median and modal levels of education were 12 and 11 years, respectively. (The level of education applies to 30 families only. We did not ask the parents' educational level for the first 50 families we interviewed.) In terms of percentage, 46.7% of the 30 parents had less than 12 years of education, 30% were high school graduates, 20% had 1 or 2 years of post–high school education (including an associate degree), and 3.3%, or one person, had a 4-year college degree.

For 60% of the families, this was the first time that they had become homeless and entered a shelter; for 32.5% of the families, this was their

TABLE 2.1 Sociodemographic Characteristics of the Sample Families

Interview unit	(n, %)
Mother only	(68, 85.0)
Father only	(3, 3.7)
Couple	(9, 11.3)

Parent's age (yrs)	
Mean (SD)	29.9 (6.04)
Median	31
Youngest	17
Oldest	49
Race (%)	
African-American	70.0
Non–Hispanic White	23.8
Hispanic	6.3
Marital status (%)	
Currently married	15.0
Cohabiting	1.3
Separated	23.7
Single/not married	60.0
Level of education (yrs)	
Mean	11.9 (1.47)
Median	12
Mode	11
Times homeless (shelter stay) (%)	
First time	60.0
Second time	32.5
Third + time/chronic	7.5
Number of times moved in the preceding 24 mo.	
Mean (SD)	2.6 (2.6)
Median	2
Mode	2
Location of own home before losing it (%)	
Inner city	75.0
Near inner city	3.8
Suburb	3.8
Rural	3.8
Other New York cities	5.0
Out of state	8.8

TABLE 2.1 *(continued)*

Number of all living children	
Mean (SD)	3.04 (1.72)
Median	3
Mode	2
Number of children at shelter with the parent(s)	
Mean (SD)	2.1 (1.38)
Median	2
Mode	1
Age of children staying at shelter	
Mean (SD)	5.87 (4.03)
Median	5.33
Parent's age at the first child's birth (yrs)	
Mean (SD)	20.10 (3.85)
Median	19
Mode	17
Under age 20	56.4%
Current source of income (%)	
None	5.0
Public assistance (PA)	61.2
Applying for PA	11.3
Earnings	5.0
PA and earnings	17.5
Work history (%)	
Currently working	6.3
In training program	8.8
Worked recently	28.8
Worked years ago	17.5
Spouse currently working or recently worked	13.8
Missing (possibly no work history)	25.0

Note: In the case of a couple, parent's characteristics refer to those of mother's.

second episode of shelter stay; and for 7.5%, or six families, they had been homeless and stayed at a shelter at least twice before this episode or their current homeless episode had lasted more than a year, although it may have been their first such episode. In other words, this group of six families includes those who appeared not to have had a stable residence of their own and to have moved from one relative's house to another or from one shelter to another. It also includes the families who lost their own home more than a year earlier but lived doubled up with a relative before they entered the shelter for the first time. The group, consisting mostly of young mothers with children and of substance abusers, may be called chronically homeless. It is to be noted that the question we asked the parents was if they had been homeless before. Without exception, the parents defined an episode of home-lessness as an episode of shelter stay and did not count doubled-up living arrangements as such.

The data on the number of times moved show that about a third of families had had pretty stable residential arrangements, meaning that they had stayed in the same apartment or house or had moved only once in the preceding 24 months. Another third had moved twice, and the rest had moved 3 times or more (as many as 15 to 20 times) in the same period, indicating that they were quite mobile or transient, either because of their own choice or because of circumstances.

In our interview, we asked the name of the street and city where they last lived in their own home and identified that 75%, or 60 families, had previously lived in inner-city neighborhoods, and 3 families had previously lived just outside the inner-city neighborhoods. Three other families had previously lived in low-income suburban areas, and 3 more in rural towns that were not far from the two cities where the shelters were located. Of the rest, 4 families had moved from other cities within New York State and 7 had moved from other states. Most of these movers also lived in inner-city or surrounding low-income neighborhoods in the cities/states from which they had moved.

As expected, a majority of these families were receiving public assis-tance (Aid to Families with Dependent Children, or AFDC, mostly, and Supplemental Security Income, or SSI, for some disabled children) as their primary income source or were in the process of applying for benefits. Only 5% of the families relied solely on earnings, and 17.5% relied on a combination of public assistance benefits and earnings. The data on work status and work history show that nearly 50% of the interviewees and/or their spouses/partners either were working at the time of the interview or had worked recently, or before they entered the shelter. As expected, most of the jobs that these people had held consisted of low-paying, unskilled work. Some were part time and/or of temporary duration; others were of long-term duration, ranging from 2 years to a number of years.

The median number of children per family staying at the shelter was 2, with a median age of 5.3 years. In addition, 7 mothers were pregnant when we interviewed them. As many as 35% of the families had at least 1 child living outside the shelter, usually in a relative's household— grandparents', father's, or aunt's. Many parents had chosen to leave their children in a relative's household to shield them from the chaotic life of a shelter and/or to enable them to continue in the same school, whereas others had given up custody of their children to their former spouse, a relative, foster care, or adoption. A few parents also told us that their teenagers were in residential treatment centers or "locked up." Older parents also had adult children living independently.

We conducted bivariate analysis to identify any significant relationship between race and any of the demographic variables that we have described above, and we found no significant racial difference. Because the interviewees constituted a nonprobability sample, we are not able to claim representativeness of any of the numbers and percentages shown in Tables 1 and 2. Thus, the results of any statistical analysis may not be meaningful. Nevertheless, the sociodemographic and economic characteristics of our sample are quite similar to those of the samples of urban homeless families investigated in previous studies.

With respect to the primary reasons for becoming homeless, 21.2% of the families listed eviction due to nonpayment of rent; 16.2% listed domestic violence; another 16.2% listed desertion by husband, divorce, and other kind of family breakup; 11.3% listed substandard housing conditions (insect/rat infestation, lack of heat and/or water, bad plumbing and/or odor); 3.8%, unscrupulous landlords (who not only rented substandard housing but also cheated their tenants out of their rent or evicted them illegally); 7.5%, drug-related crime and violence in the neighborhood; 7.5%, interviewee's own substance abuse (which led to nonpayment of rent and then to eviction or outright eviction for the problem itself); 3.8%, husband's or roommates' substance abuse; 5.0%, combination of interviewee's own substance abuse and domestic violence; 5.0%, moved to take care of an ailing parent or in search of a better job; 1.3%, chronic lack of a stable residence; and 1.3%, racial discrimination and threat from neighbors (in a low-income white suburb).

In most cases, however, this categorization was hard to do in reality, because a combination of circumstances had been responsible for the families' homelessness. For example, a majority of these families lived in substandard housing in dangerous neighborhoods; when they let go of their substandard housing, then, their desire to get out of the neighborhood played a big role in their decision. Needless to say, substandard housing and unscrupulous landlords were also hard to separate. Families did not fight illegal eviction because they thought the rental unit was inadequate anyway for lack of heat and/or water. Almost all families who were evicted for nonpayment of rent also lived in substandard units. As most families indicated, if their family economy had

TABLE 2.2 Primary Reason for Homelessness, After Losing Home and Social Support

Primary reason for homelessness (%)	
Eviction due to nonpayment of rent	21.2
Domestic violence	16.2
Desertion, divorce, and other family breakup	16.2
Substandard housing	11.3
Slumlord	3.8
Drug/crime/violence in the neighborhood	7.5
Interviewee's own substance abuse	7.5
Interviewee's substance abuse and domestic violence	5.0
Substance abuse of a family member	3.8
Moved for caregiving duties, better job	5.0
Chronic lack of a stable residence	1.3
Racial discrimination by neighbors	1.3
After losing home	
Came directly to the current shelter	33.8
Went to another shelter	7.5
Stayed at a motel	2.5
Lived on streets	1.3
Lived doubled up with	
Parent(s)	20.0
Sibling	7.5
Other relative	10.0
Friend	12.5
Friend and then relative or vice versa	5.0
Primary source of social support	
None	41.3
Parent (mostly mother)	27.5
Sibling (mostly sister)	10.1
Husband, ex-husband, or partner	7.5
Other relative	1.3
Combination of the above relatives	5.0
Friend	5.0
Church members	2.6

permitted, they would never have lived in those dangerous neighborhoods and in those substandard units. Thus, the "primary reasons" for homelessness need to be interpreted as one or more precipitating incidents that led the families, who were already vulnerable, to lose their home.

Overall, it appears that more than one fifth of the families directly attributed their homelessness to their meager economic resources, and about one fourth attributed it to substandard housing and drug-related crime- and violence-ridden inner-city neighborhood conditions and slumlords who, with their substandard rental units, took advantage of these poor families' meager resources. One sixth also attributed their homelessness to substance abuse of their own, their spouses, or room-mates with whom they had shared a house. The sinister effect of ad-dictive substances, whether played out on the streets or inside the house, as the cause of the plight of these families cannot be underesti-mated. A significant portion, or one third, of the families also attributed their homelessness to domestic violence and other relationship prob-lems. Domestic violence, which in part was also associated with sub-stance abuse, as the cause of homelessness among women and their children needs to be given special attention.

After losing or leaving their home, one third of the families had come directly to the shelter where they were staying at the time of their interview, but about one half had gone to a relative's and/or friend's and lived doubled up before they had headed to the shelter. The rest had gone to another shelter or motel or had roamed the streets before coming to the current shelter. With the exception of a few families, the doubled-up living arrangements among those who had first sought a relative's or friend's help were only short-lived, lasting for a few days to, at most, a couple of weeks. The welcome was rescinded mostly because the host families were not much better off than their homeless guests in terms of economic resources and were not able to shoulder the added burden of supporting another family. More often than not, the homeless families were the ones who voluntarily left the doubled-up living arrangements, because they were keenly aware of the predica-ment of the host family. Thus, it is not surprising to see that over 40% of the interviewed families indicated that they did not have any social support network that they would be able to lean on in times like those that they were going through.

CHARACTERISTICS OF CHILDREN
STAYING AT SHELTERS

Altogether, there were 172 children staying at three shelters with the 80 families we interviewed. Of those, 74 children, or 43%, were under age 5, 81 children, or 47%, were between ages 5 and 12, and 17 children, or 10%, were between ages 13 and 17. As shown by the data in Table

2.3, many children were reported by their parents to have a variety of health and mental health problems and developmental disabilities. The problems appeared to have been especially prevalent among school-age children, probably because the older children were more likely to have been diagnosed. For example, all 18 children reported by their parents as having asthma were school age, as were most of those reported as having lead poisoning and/or mental retardation.

Most parents also reported that their children were having a tough time adjusting to shelter life because of the trauma of losing their home and living in a congregate environment where the rules were different from those at home. Based on these parents' reports, most children showed signs of distress, with some regressing or withdrawing, whereas others became agitated and aggressive. The data under the heading "Psychosocial/Adjustment" in Table 2.3 list the number of children whose problems preexisted and had been diagnosed and whose symptoms became pronounced after they came to the shelter, to a degree that made the parents extremely concerned, as well as the number of children who developed the problems after they came to the shelter. The children whose parents wanted counseling for them included those the parents believed were traumatized by witnessing domestic or street-born violence against their mothers. Some of these children showed obvious signs of distress and trauma, whereas others did not, at least not outwardly. The "needing counseling" group also included children whose parents believed they had been maltreated by previous custodial parents/relatives.

School-age children, especially the older ones who were more likely to be aware of their environment and the stigma of being homeless, appeared to be experiencing a higher degree of emotional turmoil, although some tended to "stuff" their feelings in rather than to express them behaviorally. Added to their sense of embarrassment, shame, and stress were problems related to transportation to school and the insensitivity of teachers, school staff, and classmates who did not appear to comprehend or try to understand the homeless children's psychological needs. Moreover, some parents mentioned that their children were in dire need of other basic necessities (i.e., food and clothing), in addition to being in their own home. Meals served at shelters were not enough to meet the children's nutritional needs, and the children lacked appropriate clothes for weather and school.

The scores on the Eyberg Child Behavior Inventory that parents answered for their children ages 2 to 16 years are higher than those of normative group 2, composed of children from all classes, but they are

TABLE 2.3 Children Who Stayed in Shelters

Number of children of the 80 families who stayed at three shelters:

Total	172 (100%)
Under age 5	74 (43%)
Between ages 5 and 12	81 (47%)
Between ages 13 and 17	17 (10%)

Number of children who had the following problems (as reported by parents):

Physical/Developmental		*Psychosocial/Adjustment*	
Anemia	3	Attention deficit disorder/ hyperactivity	8
Asthma	18	Acting out/fighting	9
Blood disorder	3	Clinging to mother	7
Cancer	1	Crying/tantrum	8
Cerebral palsy	2	Sleep disorders	3
Ear, nose, or throat problem	9	Abused	5
Heart murmur	2	Withdrawal/being upset	4
Lead poisoning	7	Needing counseling	13
Migraine headache	1	*Academic/school-related*	
Mental retardation	9	Transportation	6
Over/underweight	4	Truancy	2
Ringworms	5	Lack of proper clothing	9
Skin/scalp problem	2	Being embarrassed	3
Sickle cell anemia	3	Insensitivity of teachers/ staff	5
Vision problem/blindness	4	Problems with other kids	1
Speech/hearing problem	10	Failing academically	5
Stomach disorder	2		
Seizure disorder	2		
Other (hernia, allergy, dental)	6		

almost identical to those of normative group 1, composed of domiciled children from lower and lower-middle classes.

LIMITATIONS AND STRENGTH OF THE STUDY

There are a couple of obvious limitations of this study. One is its cross-sectional design and the one-time contact with the parents, which may

**TABLE 2.4 Comparison of Scores on the Eyberg Child Behavior
           Inventory**

	Homeless children	Normative group 1	Normative group 2
n	142	512	798
Age (yr)	2–16	2–12	2–16
Income status	Extremely poor	Lower and lower-middle classes	Representative of all classes
Intensity scores			
Mean (SD)	102.9 (38.2)	103.8 (34.6)	96.6 (35.2)
Median	96	NA	NA
Problem scores			
Mean (SD)		6.9 (7.8)	7.1 (7.7)
Median		NA	NA
Ranges	0–32	0–35	NA

NA = Not available

Sources: For scores of normative group 1: Robinson, E. A., Eyberg, S. M., & Ross, A. W. (1980, Spring). The standardization of an inventory of child conduct problem behaviors. *Journal of Clinical Child Psychology*, 22–29. For scores of normative group 2: Eyberg, S. M., & Pincus, D. (In Press). *Eyberg Child Behavior Inventory and Sutter-Eyberg Student Behavior Inventory: Professional manual.* Odessa, FL: Psychological Assessment Resources. Reproduced by special permission of the publisher, Psychological Assessment Resources, Inc., 16204 North Florida Avenue, Lutz, Florida 33549, from the Eyberg Child Behavior Inventory by Sheila Eyberg, Ph.D., copyright 1974 by PAR, Inc. Further reproduction is prohibited without permission of PAR, Inc.

have placed some restrictions on the depth of our understanding of them. It certainly was not enough time to listen to their in-depth oral histories. Also, the one-time-only contact may not have been enough to establish rapport and a trusting relationship between the parents and the interviewer; as a result, the parents could have been less than completely forthcoming in answering specific questions. As mentioned earlier, another limitation is the nonprobability sampling method, which limits the generalizability of the findings. We believe, however, that these limitations are diluted by the sample size, which is large for a qualitative study. That is, in grounded theory the greater the range and the internal variety achieved by the large sample size, the greater the likelihood of external validity (Chenitz & Swanson, 1986). Overall, we do not pretend that our study represents the definitive findings on homeless families or claim its superiority to other studies of homelessness. It is in its entirety exploratory research, and the findings should be understood in that context: that the study adds another small step toward understanding the pain and suffering of homeless parents and children.

ORGANIZATION OF THE BOOK

In the remaining chapters, we follow homeless families' ordeal in chronological order. In chapter 3, we describe the circumstances preceding and the reasons for the families' homelessness. In chapter 4, we describe the families' stress caused by the doubled-up living arrangements they had experienced before they entered the shelter and their social support networks in general. In chapter 5, we describe the families' perception and experience of shelter living: the fear, relief, and gratitude when they entered the shelter; the adjustment to and challenges of the congregate living situation, including the stress of adhering to various rules, lack of privacy, despair about the present as well as the future; and, the most serious of all, parents' concerns about their children's hunger and their adjustment and academic problems. In chapter 6, we describe the frustration and barriers that these families face when trying to find decent housing. Finally, in chapter 7, we summarize our findings and recommend policies and programs that would prevent homelessness among those at risk and help homeless families to secure permanent housing. In chapters 3 through 6, we have tried to present the families' subjective perception and experience in their own words by quoting them as much as possible. We have edited the quotations only minimally for brevity and clarity.

REFERENCES

Baker, C., Wuest, J., & Stern, P. N. (1992). Method slurring: The grounded theory/ phenomenology example. *Journal of Advanced Nursing, 17*, 1355–1360.

Chenitz, W. C., & Swanson, J. M. (1986). *From practice to grounded theory.* Menlo Park, CA: Addison-Wesley.

Dash, L. (1996). *Rosa Lee: A mother and her family in urban America.* New York: Basic Books.

Habermann-Little, B. (1991). Qualitative research methodologies: An overview. *Journal of Neuroscience Nursing, 23*(3), 188–190.

Keddy, B., Sims, S. L., & Stern, P. N. (1996). Grounded theory as feminist research methodology. *Journal of Advanced Nursing, 23*, 448–453.

Kozol, J. (1988). *Rachel and her children: Homeless families in America.* New York: Crown.

Leininger, M. (1994). Evaluation criteria and critique of qualitative research studies. In J. M. Morse (Ed.), *Critical issues in qualitative research methods* (pp. 95–115). Thousand Oaks, CA: Sage.

Morse, J. M. (1994). "Emerging from the data": The cognitive processes of analysis in qualitative inquiry. In J. M. Morse (Ed.), *Critical issues in qualitative research methods* (pp. 23–45). Thousand Oaks, CA: Sage.

National Low Income Housing Coalition. (1997). *Fair market rent and poverty* [on line]. Available: www.nlihc.org/oor3.html.

Rosenthal, R. (1994). *Homeless in paradise: A map of the terrain.* Philadelphia: Temple University Press.

Sandelowski, M. (1995). Qualitative analysis: What it is and how to begin. *Research in Nursing and Health, 18,* 371–375.

Stern, P. N. (1980). Grounded theory methodology: Its uses and processes. *Image, 12*(1), 20–23.

Stern, P. N. (1994). Eroding grounded theory. In J. M. Morse (Ed.), *Critical issues in qualitative research methods* (pp. 212–223). Thousand Oaks, CA: Sage.

Strauss, A., & Corbin, J. (1990). *Basics of qualitative research: Grounded theory procedures and techniques.* Newbury Park, CA: Sage.

3

Home to Homelessness

In this chapter, we describe the circumstances that led these families to lose their home. Many families were evicted due to nonpayment of rent; many others had to let go of uninhabitable rental units because they could no longer bear the hazardous living environment; some chose to leave their substandard rental units and come to a shelter because they hoped to get into public housing; some were cheated out of their home by unscrupulous landlords who prey upon welfare checks of poor single parents; some fled to seek a refugee from drug-related vandalism and rampant violence in their poor inner-city neighborhoods; some were forced to move out because of alcohol and drug problems of family members or roommates; some had their own alcohol, drug, and/or mental health problems that resulted in the loss of their home; some fled from domestic violence; and a few had moved to fulfill their filial duty to take care of sick parents and had lost their home in the shuffle.

With the exception of a few domestic violence victims who had lived a lower-middle-class life before they fled in search of a safe place and a few others who had just hit bottom because of an unexpected turn of events in their lives, most of these families had been extremely poor and lived in a precarious housing situation even before they eventually lost their home. For a significant proportion of them, this episode of homelessness was not their first. Given that, for most of them, the household head's educational attainment was poor, with only 11 years of schooling, on average, and work histories were minimal, these families may never be able to escape poverty. As poverty breeds all kinds of problems, most of these families had lived with the weight of multiple problems for a long period (many of them since childhood). Almost all families who had been evicted for nonpayment of rent had been living in substandard units in poor, crime-ridden neighborhoods. The homelessness of other families could be attributed to the combination of poverty, substance abuse and/or mental health problems, and abusive relationships. Thus, it is hard to pinpoint a singular and specific cause of their homelessness, although we tried to sort out, in the paragraph above, the immediate circumstances that triggered their homelessness, as described by the families.)

In presenting their subjective perception and evaluation of the circumstances under which they lost their home, however, we would still like to highlight the internal heterogeneity behind the face of homeless families as well as the common vulnerability that these families have been subject to due to extreme poverty.

By "internal heterogeneity," we mean the different paths by which these families fell from the domiciled state to the homeless state—meager paychecks, unemployment, disability, desertion by the breadwinner-husband, meager public assistance benefits, desire for freedom and independence from an abusive partner, addiction, and so forth. In our interviews with the family head(s), we realized that these distinctions were important to them and that not all of them shared the same perceptions or feelings about homelessness. Over and over, we heard them pronounce, "*I am not an addict, have never been, and I don't want to be treated like one*"; "*This is a new beginning for me; I am here to start a new life for me and my children*"; "*I have never been homeless before*"; or "*I have always been able to provide a roof over their [children's] heads.*" In many cases, they tried to disassociate themselves from the mass of the homeless and yearned to be viewed as a family that was temporarily down/in the dumps because of their specific circumstances. For these families, it is important to keep a continuity in their identity as who they had been before they became homeless, because homelessness implies a shameful failure and the families feel stigmatized by it. For other household heads, especially those who had fled from an abusive spouse/partner, homelessness, though painful, represents their courage, not a failure, and a point for a fresh start. Yet others, especially those who have become homeless repeatedly, appeared to have accepted homelessness as a part of life that is beyond their control. Each family indeed has different needs, and social service providers must treat each family as a separate, independent entity.

Despite these disparate reasons for becoming homeless and perceptions of homelessness, these families had, more often than not, shared similar consequences of extreme poverty before they entered an emergency shelter. Most importantly, the ravages of poverty made them more vulnerable to negative external forces such as urban decline, infusion of illegal substances, and crime than the nonpoor, mostly because of their residential segregation in poor urban areas where these forces are in full action. It appears that poverty also made them more susceptible to domestic violence, family breakup, and family disputes than their nonpoor counterparts, because poverty by its nature does not allow continuity and tends to create instability. Thus, the lives of these families before they entered a shelter have had common threads of victimization by these negative forces, instability in physical environment, work opportunity, and family life, and the constant struggle to protect the children from these destructive forces and keep the family together. When we deal with issues of homelessness, then, we must not forget these insidious environments and the constant struggle that these families have engaged on a daily basis.

In the following, we present families who were evicted for nonpayment of rent and/or other reasons (the evicted), and families who fled, by choice or by the force of circumstances, to seek a refuge from domestic and/or drug-related violence and other environmental conditions hazardous even for a bare minimum standard of living (refuge seekers). We also present families who were caregivers and families who appeared to have moved frequently in a vain search for a better life (movers/wanderers).

THE EVICTED

The most frequently given reason for losing their home was eviction due to nonpayment of rent. Most families felt that their rent was too high for their income, whether public assistance, a Social Security check, or a paycheck, and for the usually substandard quality of housing and the undesirable neighborhood where it was located. The immediate circumstances under which families got behind in paying their rent, however, were quite diverse.

The Welfare Poor

A large proportion of the interviewed homeless families had depended on public assistance (Aid to Families with Dependent Children [AFDC] or Supplemental Security Income [SSI]) as their primary, if not sole, source of income. Some worked part time to supplement their welfare check, but the minimum-wage jobs they worked were mostly temporary. Although New York granted these poor families a check more generous than that in most other states, the welfare check, even when supplemented by an occasional paycheck, was still not enough to cover the basic necessities of food, shelter, and clothing. These families lived on the edge, and any small crisis, such as a check that arrived late or was for a reduced amount, could easily lead them to become homeless.

Paula and John, both in their early 20s, a married couple with three young children, described the problems that led them to lose their apartment 3 months ago: "*Downtown [County Department of Social Services—DSS] had sent my rent late. He [landlord] didn't get it to the first half of the month in June. He asked that if we didn't have our rent by the first of the month that we be gone. We didn't want to get evicted, so we left on our own will. Downtown was messing us up on our money. My husband was working, and they cut the money and the rent. And in August she [caseworker] wasn't gonna pay the rent because they said we were making enough from his salary. He worked part time, like 32 hours a week, never more than 35, at Red Apple, you know, the convenience stores. He was only bringing home like a hundred and twenty dollars. . . . I am trying to get off of public assistance so bad. I'm so sick of the system. They are messing around a lot. My caseworker is so nasty.*" They went to Paula's mother's house, but the mother told them to get out. Paula was going to a vocational school at that time.

Brenda, a 31-year-old single mother of six, lost her house 10 months earlier in Virginia: "*We were evicted. I lost my ID—my Social Security card. Someone found it and got a job with it, and I didn't get a check for a month. When I called them [DSS], they said you didn't get a check because you got a job. I told them I didn't and that I lost my ID. They said I had to come down and sign papers. I did, but I was already 1 month behind in my rent. The landlord didn't even want to see a statement that I would be getting my money. So, we had to go.*" Brenda had been homeless before: "*I was in the [homeless shelter] in Virginia about 2 years ago. I was staying with a friend, and we got in an argument. She told me I could leave and the kids could stay. If I'm leaving, my kids are leaving too. So I had paid her my money. She called the police. The police told her different things she could do. So I said 'I'll just live on the street.' I didn't want to go to a shelter. They said if we see you sleeping on the street, we'll take the kids. So I went to the [shelter]. I was there for about 3 months.*"

Debby, a 32-year-old single mother who stayed at a shelter with her 8-year-old daughter, was on welfare and was also working on and off:

"*I owed the landlady back rent. I had lived there for about 3 years. Then I had lent my girlfriend some money because she thought she could give it right back to me when her boyfriend came back home. And then he said he wouldn't have no money till the next week and stuff, and that really messed me up. I had no money. . . . Yeah, I was working for this temporary service. They call me when they have work available. Then they called me and I had bus fare for the whole week, and I had gotten off the last shift and no bus came. I waited for more than an hour and a half and finally called the public transit office. They told me the bus service stopped some hours ago. I had to catch a cab with my bus fare. The next morning I called the agency to see if I could get an earlier shift, and they said, 'You just can't come back,' because, you see, every time they gave me the job, I had transportation problems.*" Following the eviction, Debby and her daughter stayed with Debby's cousin for a while.

Michelle, a 28-year-old mother of five, had moved to a trailer in a suburban area about 40 minutes away from the inner city where she grew up because she did not want her children in the city. She lived there for 2 years before the trailer she was renting was foreclosed: "*I had a month to find an apartment, but in the suburbs there wasn't much for the money that I could afford. I came to the city and stayed with my mother for a couple of weeks. . . . You never think it [homelessness and shelter living] will happen, but it does.*"

Wilma is a 41-year-old mother of two grown children (living independently) and a 9-year-old. She, with Jim, her husband of 18 years sitting next to her, described their situation: "*Our rent was late because I was in the hospital over the summer; I am a manic depressive. When I got out, I went to pay our rent, and they [the landlord family] said they already started eviction proceedings. We went to court and they told us to pay the late rent, and I said, 'OK.' The utility bill was due on the 30th, and I am on Social Security disability and I don't get my check until the 3rd. So, I went to pay them on the third and they wouldn't accept it, so now we are here. I talked to my lawyer and she said to just leave. She said they would just keep on hassling us. And the drug traffic and all. They still have my security deposit of $440.*"

Karen, a 32-year-old widow with two children, also had trouble because her landlord changed the rules and wanted the rent payment by the first of every month, not on the third, when her Social Security check comes. The landlord would not allow her to pay half the rent on the first and the other half on the 3rd. He took her security deposit for the month's rent and evicted the family. It appears that some landlords impose an unreasonable demand on these poor families as a means of evicting them, either because the families are undesirable tenants or because the landlord would like to raise the rent. Karen had lived in shelters off and on since her 11-year-old mentally retarded, hyperactive son was born. (Her 14-year-old daughter lives with the girl's grandmother.) Karen had been previously jailed, and she appeared to have some mental health as well as developmental disability problems. The family also had dealings with the child protective services. These factors certainly do not endear the family to many landlords.

David is a proud, 49-year-old father of 3- and 4-year-old boys. He has five grown children from his previous marriage to a woman who has become well known for her work with domestic violence victims. He is very proud and protective of his ex-wife's reputation. ("*People know her, and I don't think I want to use her name.*") He had worked for the New York City school system for 26 years and the parks department for 11 years (when school was out) before he retired on disability. His 3-year-old was born to a crack-addicted mother, and his 4-year-old is not his but his son's half brother whom he adopted. Ever since the 3-year-old was born prematurely and abandoned by his mother, David has taken care of him and has been granted full custody. ("*I went [to see the baby at a hospital] everyday for 3 months on my lunch. . . . I felt like I hit the Lotto when I walked out of that hospital with him. People said in 20 years they have never seen a man walk out with a baby, never a man.*") Two years ago, after David retired on disability, he moved his family of three to Buffalo to "*give them [the boys] a better education and life*" and to be close to his grown daughter. Two months ago, he lost his apartment:

"*I get workmen's compensation and Social Security Disability. My workmen's compensation was delayed from August 19 to September 30. Even though I could have paid my rent when my Social Security came, I bought my children clothes and school stuff because they were starting school in September. I had no knowledge my [workmen's compensation] checks would be late after 4 years of coming every 2 weeks. . . . The day before I was gonna get locked out by the marshal, I found out about this shelter; somebody told me about it. I got things for my kids, stuff that they need when it gets cold here, and I came here at 8:30 in the morning, and they told me I couldn't be a walk-in. I had to call in. So I made an appointment at 9:30, and I have been here since then.*"

Overall, the precariousness of living on the edge is a constant for most families who depend on government checks, especially paltry public assistance payments for their living. Andrea, a 26-year-old mother of three, sums it up: "*Stability, that's been a big problem ever since I had my son. I go downtown [DSS], and they tell me I get $205 for an apartment and there aren't any for $205. I know I am on public assistance and I have* *to do without things, but come on. We want a floor we can walk on. It's ridiculous. My apartment costs more, so I fall short on other things. I was brought up where my parents did OK, and now I can't get to a point where things are good. I am in a job and I spend $15 too much and my apartment is gone. . . . I don't want to be flipping hamburgers all my life. If I have to, I will. With me going to school [community college], it showed my kids it was important. But, I haven't been to school since Thursday. We can miss only so many days and I already missed four days before this. . . . So now it's like 'what do I do?' School is all I got. Flipping burgers won't teach my kids anything."*

The Unemployed Poor

Like families on welfare, most poor working families live from hand to mouth. Their meager paychecks do not allow them room to save for emergencies or rainy days ahead. When they lose their job, most of them cannot afford to pay rent for that very month. And the jobs they work at are not stable, with workers subject to frequent layoffs from one job after another.

Sandy and her husband, Aaron, both 38 years old, moved to Rochester from New York City in search of a better job. In Rochester, Aaron got into trouble with the law and was put on probation but was still able to keep his job. Sandy sent their three children back to New York City to be in the care of Aaron's mother and moved to Buffalo to work at a job. As soon as Aaron finished his probation, he and the children were soon to follow her to Buffalo. But she lost her apartment 2 months ago: *"I lost my job (it was a factory sort of place making notebooks and binders for colleges and stuff), and my husband got laid off. So, we haven't been able to catch up for that one month. It didn't really make sense to stay there [a one-bedroom apartment] because we needed a bigger place. Yeah, my children just came from New York City, and we couldn't stay there because it was small. I was paying $350, and the whole apartment was probably the size of this room. The children were staying with my mother-in-law till they finished their school year. Somebody said, 'Go over to the shelter, you may get more help, a place that's more affordable.' So that's what we did."*

When Sandy lost her job and subsequently the apartment, Aaron came to Buffalo to see her, in violation of his probation. For that reason, Aaron was in jail at the time we interviewed Sandy.

Marian works at a school cafeteria during the school year. During the summers, when school is out, she must find another job to support her

15-year-old son and herself. She had always been successful in finding summer jobs until the summer when we met her:

"I got evicted. My landlord raised my rent and I couldn't afford it. . . . Yeah, it was $50 more, and I couldn't make it. I lost my job because I only work when there is school. I got $140 in food stamps and about $275 every 2 weeks from work. . . . No, he [landlord] was cutting me slack; I was in a cute little cottage for $250. He was good with me; he even tried to get me jobs . . . he was kind; there aren't many like him. But he went up on the rent by $50; I couldn't do it. It was cute but not too great. Plus the area is getting real wild with drugs and people hurting one another. . . . My job with the Board of Education, I have to find me a job in the summer when there is no school. The kids are taking all the good jobs, to make money and stay out of trouble. So I couldn't find me a job; it's not like I wasn't looking. . . . I tried to get public assistance, and they denied me assistance. No medical assistance for my son [who is asthmatic], nothing for us at all. They say I work 10 months for the Board. And I am not eligible for unemployment either."

Before the current shelter admitted both family members, Marian went to stay with a friend while her son went to a shelter for homeless youth. Marian was very worried about her son: *"Yeah, he's a good kid. He's been going to [a magnet school for honors students] since the fifth grade, and now he is in tenth and this is taking a toll on him."*

Marie, 27 years old, and Sean, 31 years old, are a married couple with three children ages 7 years, 4 years, and 11 months. They used to have a lower-middle-class life on Sean's earnings as an accountant in a different city. When they moved to Buffalo to be close to Marie's mother, he had difficulty finding a job that paid as much:

"We worked at [a nonprofit urban service organization]. We worked. He worked as an accountant at different places. He really didn't get a big break here because he used to work in the accounting department of a hotel in Columbia, South Carolina. That's where he is now. He left 4 days ago. So it was really hard to get that sort of break when he came here. And then things just went downhill for a while."

The family stayed with Marie's mother for a while in her one-bedroom apartment. Marie's sister was already living with her mother. Soon Marie and Sean had difficulty with each other *"because I was getting much depressed and stressed out, and my husband was already depressed because of the failure of his job."* Sean went to stay with his sister for a while, and Marie and the children moved to the shelter. Sean went back to Columbia hoping that he could return to his old job and move his family back.

The Working Poor

Even when a parent is working, the meager paycheck from a minimum-wage job cannot fill the holes in a poor family's financial situation. Sooner or later, the hole becomes too big to mend and an unexpected emergency can cause a working poor family to become homeless.

Jacqueline and Tony, both 20 years old, are married and have a 7 1/2-month-old baby. They previously worked at minimum-wage jobs in a mall. When they lost their car because they did not have enough money to keep it repaired, they lost both their jobs and their apartment. Since they came to the shelter directly, Tony started to work again. However, the lack of transportation and day care prevented Jacqueline from going back to work, and they were still at a shelter, trying to find housing in the suburbs. They were determined not to go back to the city for the sake of the baby.

"We moved out to [a suburb] because I don't want my child to grow up in the city, and we rented a house [for the past 6 months], which racked up our bill by another $200. By the time we finished paying off car payments, paid the rent, put food on the table, and bought the baby's necessities, we didn't have enough money to fix the brakes when the car went. We lost our vehicle, so we both lost our jobs and just started heading downhill. . . . It only takes him [Tony] a couple of days to find another job, but for the pay that he needs to support all three of us, paying rent, putting food on the table, and buying the baby's necessities, there's not a lot of jobs. . . . Yeah, it would help out a lot more if there were two incomes, not one, but it costs about $130 a week for day care, so that's the whole paycheck right there, if not more. And we can't pay car insurance, and half the time we can't pay the phone bills. . . . It gets frustrating because you get to a certain point where you think, 'OK, you are getting there; you are almost there.' Then you don't have insurance, so you can't get [the baby] to the doctors, and you know it's wall after wall and you can't get anywhere."

Carol, 25 years old, and Brian, 27 years old, are a married couple with three children, ages 8, 5, and 1. They both had some postsecondary education. Carol has been working as a nurse's aide 30 hours a week for 4 years, and Brian has worked for a roofing company but now washes dishes in a restaurant full time. Seven months ago, the couple decided to split up and each went separate ways; Carol and the children went to her mother's, and Brian went to his brother's. Before they left for their relatives' homes, their apartment in an inner-city neighborhood was also robbed: *"It was missing a lot of items."* When they decided to resolve their differences and get back together, they found a major obstacle, lack of money to find new housing. Brian told their story: *"She*

[Carol] was at her mother's and paying expenses there, so she couldn't save money, and I was at my brother's, also giving him money, so I couldn't save either. We have to build ourselves back up. The rent is like $500 to $600 for the neighborhood we want to live in. Most are only two bedrooms. We are looking for a four bedroom. If utilities are all included with the rent, it would be livable, but that is not usually the case. We have to budget for utilities, then see how much rent we can afford."

Carol works during the day, and Brian works a night shift so that they do not have to worry about child care and are able to save enough money for a security deposit and the first month's rent.

Chris and Andy, 31 and 33 years old, are also married with three children, ages 10, 8, and 2. Andy works as a tow truck driver, and Chris is a homemaker. When Andy, who had a gambling problem, left the family for a while, Chris did not have any financial resources to pay the rent on time:

"We got evicted for not paying rent. He [Andy] took off and didn't leave me any money, and we were like 2 days behind the rent. I didn't know where he was or nothing. We stayed at a motel for a couple of weeks, then we went to my brother's, and then we went back to the motel for about a month. When we came to the shelter, I called around and told him I was at the shelter, so he came here."

They were having a hard time finding an apartment in a neighborhood that was *"fit for kids."*

Jill, a 35-year-old mother of four (the oldest one is in college in a different state), used to be self-sufficient, employed as a day care worker, before she moved to Buffalo:

"I had a house fire in California, and I went through homelessness there. I didn't want to get any help there or find any shelter; I didn't know where the shelters were. I was born and raised in Buffalo, so it was strange. I didn't have any information. I didn't know where to go. My sister came to town and realized what kind of shape I was in, so she made arrangements for me to come and stay with her in Illinois until I can get my IDs back because I lost a lot of things in the fire—even my documents. I had to get everything from my Social Security card to all my ID. I had to search for hospital records. It took about 3 months. Then I came to Buffalo, and my mother took the kids and put them in school. I came here [Buffalo] in March, and at the time I had no income. I couldn't even get a job at the time, and I was trying to locate a home for my children. Mom and I have had our differences off and on. I guess when I came here I was dealing with a lot of negative issues, and I had a lot of trouble getting information on how I could get a house. I didn't know what agency or service to go to. My brother, who knew about some agencies, suggested I come here."

The Poor with Substance Abuse Problems

Addiction would wreak havoc on anyone, regardless of financial situation, but its economic impact is especially harsh for the poor. Judy, a 27-year-old single mother of three, Annette, a 32-year-old single mother of three, and Colleen, a 32-year-old mother of four (she had the custody of the youngest one only; the other children live with her ex-husbands or her mother) all admitted that their drug and/or drinking habit caused them to lose their apartment: "*I was using drugs [and/or drinking] and not paying my rent and got evicted for it.*" Georgia and Doug, a married couple in their 30s, have had drinking problems that resulted in foster care placement of all four of their children. When they "*got out of the rehab, the landlord changed the locks.*" Sue, a 32-year-old mother of a teenage daughter, and her drug dealer-partner were arrested in a raid: "*One of the stipulations of my probation is that I stay away from drugs, drug dealers, drug addicts, and so forth. And the house I was living in was a known drug house, and I couldn't live there anymore. So I had to pack it up and move here. I could have stayed in the house, but I didn't want my officer coming out on an unexpected house visit, and my friend [who went to jail] left me with her 14-year-old daughter, her 17-year-old boyfriend, and their 3-month-old baby. It was just too much.*"

Judy has been working as a part-time school bus aide for the past 9 years, and this was the first time she had become homeless. Unlike Judy, however, most of those who were evicted because of their substance abuse problems had previously been homeless for the same reason and had no source of income other than public assistance. In the case of Colleen, her drug addiction and alcoholism as well as domestic abuse had been responsible for four more episodes of homelessness in the preceding 2 years while she was in and out of rehab services. Annette, also a domestic violence victim, had alternated between shelters and "*roaming the street*" for the previous "*five or six months*" alone. Nevertheless, some still did not neglect to tell us that they had been good citizens before they fell into the trap of addictive substances and accompanying problems. For example, Sue told us that she had worked for 11 years as a home care aide and 3 years as a certified nursing assistant at a respected local nursing home. Michael, a 36-year-old single father of two, says: "*I worked for [a famous company]. I was working as a cashier for a national drugstore. But when my son [a 5-year-old] was sexually assaulted, I almost had a nervous breakdown. It took a toll on everything. I lost my job, lost my house; I started using drugs. I lost it, everything. I was on a path to success, but then it all blew up. . . .*" Michael moved to a nearby town to seek support from his family, but found that his family *"was kind of into thug life. So some of them ended up in jail."* He and his 5-year-old fled from the family's drug problems and arrests and moved at least six times in the preceding 24 months, including stays in two shelters.

Even if these poor people pay their rent on time, substance abuse problems make them undesirable tenants. Sonia, who works as a receptionist at a podiatrist's office, explains why she lost her apartment: *"The lease was up. She [the landlady] didn't give an option to renew it. It's a long story. The guy I was living with had problems. He was drunk. Every time he got drunk, we would argue and he would call the police; he said it was for my protection. He never hit me or laid a hand on me. But the police was always there, and the landlady got tired of it, although she didn't live below us or anything. When the lease was up, she said I could live there on a month-by-month basis. Then 2 days later she said, 'You have to get out.'"*

Without continuous treatment and supervision, parents with substance abuse problems have difficulty staying even in transitional housing. Wendy, a 29-year-old single mother of one, had been placed in rehab transitional housing but was evicted because of her continuing problem: *"Well, on the lease, I didn't read it too well. On the lease it said if I was caught drinking or using any substance, then I would be kicked out. So I was drinking a couple of weeks ago and got kicked out."* Wendy's case underscores the importance of a supportive housing environment that incorporates treatment and close supervision of parents who have substance abuse problems. Without these supportive services, they are at risk of going through the revolving door of homelessness.

The Deserted and Divorced Poor

Relationship problems drove many poor women and their children to homelessness, because they had been totally dependent on their husband or partner for daily living. Many working women also find it impossible to maintain their own apartment on their income alone when they and their spouse/partner part ways. One of the most wrenching situations was that of 29-year-old Yolanda and her four children, ages 11 through 4:

"Initially my husband got out of the military and he was truck driving, and then he just stopped. He decided he just didn't want to be with the family. He wouldn't send any money. He had been gone for 5 months, and then I couldn't manage no more. The Crisis Center was helping, and my son—he's chronic asthmatic—went into ICU, and I couldn't make it. . . . I

would borrow from people. Eventually I had to go and apply for public assistance [in Georgia]. Then we moved to Buffalo [to be with her father, aunt, and sister] and stayed with my sister for 2 days and then came to the shelter. This is a change for the kids. They were military brats. We lived in government quarters for years and if we had to live off post, my husband took care of it. . . . I was taken care of, and this is new to me too."

Another one was Renee, a 29-year-old mother of a 5-year-old: "*[Three and a half years ago] I knew something was wrong in the marriage. I could tell, a woman can tell that some things are wrong. . . . My husband cheated on me and refused to come clean about it, so I asked for a separation and told him to get out. I stayed in the apartment for about another month, but I couldn't afford it [on her earnings as a bookkeeper in a dentist's office]. So I went to live with my mother, and I've been there ever since, up until this point in time. I was in the hospital 2 weeks, and I decided I didn't want to go back to my mother's after speaking with someone from public assistance. They told me that it would hurt my chance of being able to get on public assistance, and so I decided that this would be the best move for me because I really am homeless. I didn't feel that there was anyplace else I could go. I am going to be on PA and looking for my own apartment and get back to work eventually."*

Rebecca, a 29-year-old mother of two, said: "*We were married, and he bought the house. . . . I was a toll collector, working at the New York State toll booths. I ended up leaving that because he's a minister and he passed his own church and I was the first lady. And he got to complaining that it's important that the first lady be at church on Sunday mornings. So I took a leave of absence and eventually quit the job for him. . . . When we were divorced, he told me he wasn't able to continue paying the mortgage payments, and so we decided we were going to sell the house. But eventually, I found out he wanted the house for him and his new wife. He's staying there now, and I ended up here. . . . "*

While Rebecca stayed at the shelter, the children stayed with their father. Fortunately, she found a job after only 4 days at the shelter: "*It's medical office work, because I graduated with a diploma for medical secretary and also a degree for medical assistant. But I'm waiting to take the state exam to be certified because I want to work in a hospital, not a doctor's office, and you need to be certified for that.*" Because of her educational background, Rebecca's homeless episode was going to be very short. She hoped to be reunited with her children as soon as she could find an apartment. Meantime, she was seeing them by visiting them at school.

Pamela, a 28-year-old mother of a 15-month-old boy, explained that when she and her partner, both paraprofessionals in human services, ended their 7-year relationship, she did not have a place for herself and her son. Many homeless women told us similar stories.

Eviction Due to Racial Bias

Some African-American interviewees said that the color of their skin was a barrier to finding good housing in a decent neighborhood, and some white interviewees said that they did not want to live in predominantly black neighborhoods (see chapter 5). But not many said that their race or ethnicity was a factor in losing their apartment. Whether or not the interviewees felt uncomfortable talking to us about the subject is not clear. Largely because most of the African-American families had lived in racially segregated inner-city neighborhoods, their race per se did not figure as a factor in their homelessness. Thus, Amanda's experience, described below, is unique among those we interviewed. Amanda, who is African-American, lived with her three children ages 5 years to 11 months, whose father is white, in a blue-collar white suburb that had developed notoriety for the racial bias of some of its residents.

"I got hit by a motorcycle in August. It was a hit and run. And then I started having a lot of racial problems: people taping notes to our door, 'Niggers must leave or die,' that type of stuff. I guess the landlord didn't appreciate the fact that I called the cops several times. I guess it was from me calling the police station, and he said that he pays the water [swimming pool] for his tenants only, because my nieces and nephews used to come over and get in the pool and he didn't like it. The eviction went through, but he had to take me to court. I knew it wasn't legitimate and I had a case, but I just didn't go all through with it."

Amanda told us that she had chosen to live in the suburb for the sake of her children's education; there was just no way she would send her children to an inner-city public school. (At the shelter, she was home schooling her daughter.) The circumstances under which she had become homeless point to the reality that racism is a significant barrier as much as poverty for poor blacks, especially single parents on welfare, to find housing outside inner-city neighborhoods. Even for Amanda, who was determined as well as brave to venture into a white suburb, her neighbors' hostility was too much to bear.

THOSE WHO FLED

A majority of our homeless families had their previous addresses in dilapidated, often racially segregated, inner-city neighborhoods. The poor condition of the houses and apartments in which they had lived was caused by years of neglect of proper maintenance by absentee landlords. Apparently, building inspectors look the other way, because they think that it is not worth investing money in these old rundown places and that many landlords are likely to be eager to foreclose after collecting as much rent as possible. It also appears that many unscrupulous landlords take advantage of poor welfare recipients by renting them substandard units. The county DSS sends rent checks directly to landlords who sign a contract, so they are guaranteed rent payments for their tenants. Because the DSS pays relatively low rent, the units that are signed up for the rent contract are often the most rundown.

The quality of life of these poor families is further eroded by rampant drug-related vandalism and other crimes in their neighborhoods. Parents, siblings, husbands, partners, and roommates become substance abusers and drive the poor families to homelessness. Alcohol and drug abuse as well as the stress that results from harsh life circumstances also appear to be significant factors contributing to domestic violence against these poor women.

Substandard Housing and Unresponsive Landlords

Most of the time, families in substandard housing endured uninhabitable living conditions for years before they left the place either because they could no longer endure it or because coming to a shelter was their only chance to find better housing in a public housing project or to receive Section 8 vouchers.

Betty, a 33-year-old single parent of a 9-year-old, says: "*The plumbing upstairs was bad, and it was draining down into my apartment and I had to empty buckets of waste. . . . The landlord? He didn't come over and see about it. He didn't come fix it. I moved in wintertime, and it wasn't leaking then. As the weather got warmer, it started leaking and just dripping, just a little bit. I told him about it, and then after it got even hotter, it started to . . . like a constant drip. Then it started stinking. A real bad stench as the house being closed up every day, me going to work every day, it got to be a little too much.*"

Betty and her daughter stayed with Betty's sister for a week before they came to the shelter.

Angela, her husband, and their three children left their apartment because the children, especially the 19-month-old twins, were bitten by bugs and ants and they "*just couldn't take it no more.*" They had stayed at a motel for 2 days and at a welfare hotel for 3 days before they came to the shelter. In addition to the bug problems, the family were afraid in the unsafe surroundings. Angela described her fear in the situation that made the family let go of the apartment: "*I saw people getting killed up in their own house, and I was terrified of being by myself because my husband used to work a night job from 11:00 to 7:00 or 8:00 in the morning.*"

Denise described a lack of water and a falling ceiling, Fred recalled roach infestation and a bad animal odor, Linda had water pipe problems and a lack of heat ("*We practically froze*"), and Samantha and Noreen, among other things, faced big rats and a broken heater, causing them to leave their apartments. Noreen said: "*It was one of the worst apartments. . . . He [the landlords' son and Noreen's acquaintance] and another guy used to live upstairs, and when I visited him it was neat. But there were a lot of things I didn't see. Rat holes. One day my daughter sat watching TV, and there was a big rat, walking along. My children were terrified. . . . I was raised in the ghetto, in the [name of the streets] area, and we lived around those sort of things. But I won't have my children living around that. After a month, I told them [the landlords] that I wasn't giving them no more money.*"

Others asked their landlords to fix the problems to no avail. Jennifer, a 24-year-old with a 9-month-old baby, described her apartment: "*The place was infested with rats. He [the landlord] took advantage of me because I was a young single woman. Before my baby's father and I fell out, he'd tell the landlord. But when it was just me, he [the landlord] wouldn't do anything.*" Esther believes that her landlord did not turn the heat on "*because the heat was included in the rent.*" She also had water damages, and the house was broken into: "*We had ongoing problems with the landlord.*"

Tammy, a 33-year-old divorced mother of three, ages 9, 8, and 7 years, vividly describes the condition of her apartment and the behavior of a slumlord who illegally forced her family out of the apartment:

"*I told the [director of the shelter] the other day that they ought to start a list of landlords that just screw people that are on public assistance. They know that they can get away with it. Let me tell you about this apartment. I am so mad. Now mind you, I moved into this place in March or April of last year. I lived in the back house, and then when I moved into the upstairs, it wasn't even cleaned. The people who had lived there before me, their garbage was still sitting there after 6 months. It stunk. I had to clean it, OK? Then I lived there a couple of months, and the bottom [unit] came open, so I moved there for a couple of months; then the front came open and I moved in. He [the landlord] did the same kind of eviction with her [another tenant] as he did me now. I moved in, and he said he would fix what was wrong within a week. My kitchen sink I had to plunge every time*"

I did dishes because the water would stay there; there was silverware and stuff down in the pipes. In the bathroom the tiling was coming apart, and there was plaster behind it that would come off every time my kids would take a bath. My bathroom sink was ready to come off the wall; there was no ceiling in the bathroom. Half-painted rooms; no screens on any of the windows; no storm windows. Some of the windows actually had bullet holes in them. There were holes in the bedroom walls, where they had put in new pipes and never filled it in. My back door had a huge crack in it where someone had tried to break in, and none of this stuff ever got fixed. Four hundred dollars a month for this, and I had to pay my own utilities on top of it. And then my landlord puts in a coin-operated washer and dryer, and they were running on my electric bill, $189 a month. I told him I wasn't going to pay it no more, and I think that's why he got rid of me. Something I was going to report him about, you know. Winter last year I had to call the Health Department because he took the controls away from me, and my apartment was 58 degrees all winter long. My kids were sick and he won't turn it up because the gas was in his name. I had the Health Department come out, and I think that's why he had us leave. . . . And what galls me is that I haven't been gone barely and he's got someone else living in there on public assistance, and he's gonna do it again, he's gonna do it again. That's two families he's done that to. And this is a 24-year-old man. His dad owns like eight or nine properties. So it was just, I'm glad I'm out of there, but I'm not glad that I don't have a place of my own."

Tammy had gone to court and received an injunction for a month's stay against the landlord's illegal immediate eviction notice, but the landlord would not respect the court order: "*Yeah, a full month and when I got this piece of paper from housing that had the law on it, I handed it to him, the landlord, and these were his words—quote 'I don't give a shit what the law says, make sure you're out today' unquote—and threw it back to me.*" She told us that she called the police when the landlord was verbally abusive to her and pushing her out of the apartment and that the police would not show up in time. When the police finally arrived, they told Tammy that they could not do anything because the landlord was not present. The landlord sped away in his car as the police car was pulling in: "*You know, the cops told me I can stay, but I didn't. I've got a lot of physical problems right now, and I just, I couldn't deal with it. I couldn't deal with it anymore, so I figured it was my best interest emotionally to just go, you know. And hope and pray that somewhere, I'd get some place. And I got lucky, I got here.*"

In fact, some landlords were blatantly cheating their poor tenants who received rent subsidies from the DSS. Lauren and her husband, with three children, were evicted by one such slumlord: "*He said he didn't cash the two-party check for the rent, but he did. He cashed the check and forged my signature when I lived there for 2 months. Then he gave us an eviction notice with only 3 days to leave."*

As mentioned, for many, coming to a shelter was also a means to facilitate their admission to a public housing project or their application for public assistance benefits. Apparently, some of those interviewed had come to believe that the benefits of a homeless shelter outweigh the stigma of staying there. Homeless shelters were seen as a gateway to better and more desirable housing and a conduit to a public assistance system, although not everyone who hoped to reap such benefits by entering the shelter system was guaranteed the benefits. Mary said: *"Actually, it wasn't that I lost it [the apartment]. It was my decision to leave the apartment because of rats and mice. Plus, I didn't like the neighborhood. I didn't have a doorknob, and there was some work to be done. I had spoken to him [the landlord], and he said he would come but never came and there was no one living downstairs and I didn't feel very comfortable. I figured if I came here, I could make it into [public housing] quicker, because everything [such as utilities] is included. It didn't turn out that way. I wasn't lucky enough to get one [public housing]."*

Some public housing projects located in the dilapidated inner-city neighborhoods are dangerous places to live because of drugs and drug-related violence. Nonetheless, most homeless families wanted to get into public housing for economic reasons because rent, including utility, is proportional to their income and maintenance is included. In other words, unlike private-sector rental units, public housing units at least offer them residential stability, regardless of fluctuations in their income. Parents like Mary, who have been completely at the mercy of the vagaries of minimum-wage jobs, needed the benefits of public housing. Pregnant with her third child, Mary described the instability of her job: *"I was working where Freezer Queen is, doing assembly work on the line. I was there approximately 30 or 32 hours a week. It depended, because they would lay you off one day and maybe call you back. It varied. I've also done light industrial, clerical, telemarketing with temporary agencies. I stopped working when I was about 2 months pregnant; my back started bothering me from standing up all day. I wouldn't mind getting a part-time job, though."*

Linda, who had to leave because of broken water pipes and a lack of heat, said: *"The landlord didn't try to get anything done, and I had another baby coming, so I left and came here. I could have gone to my mother's house, but people recommended I come here so I can get back on benefits [PA]. I had a sanction for 6 months because I worked then. I was laid off since. They didn't give my daughter anything either, so I didn't have any-*

thing from downtown [DSS] for 10 months. It was hard, so I came here. I had to have my own house, so I hoped that coming here would speed things up. I get more help here and help with the security deposit. My unemployment [insurance] didn't come till February. Unemployment until July, $95 a week, isn't enough to take care of me and my two kids. I haven't had food stamps in the last 10 months either. Now that I have my second child, it will be harder."

Most families who left substandard housing had lived in a similar environment for a number of years. That is, the inner-city rental units they could get into were largely substandard, and they had faced many of the same problems before. Moreover, many rented apartment buildings or multiplex houses in those poor neighborhoods are built so close to each other that tenants who live in them often face serious fire hazards. For example, Linda told us that her previous episode of homelessness was due to a fire in the apartment across from hers that left her apartment without heat and gas. She was lucky that she was not hurt.

Victims of Drug-Related Crime and Violence in the Neighborhood

The poor neighborhoods where most of the homeless families rented their housing were often infested with drug dealers, drug-related vandalism, and violence, including gang activities. Parents had been extremely worried about their and their children's safety. Many of them said, "*I just had to leave*" because violence threatened their daily lives, and they said they had been "*continuously running from the same thing, drug infested areas.*" Many homeless families expressed that staying at shelters was much safer than staying in their previous homes in those neighborhoods.

Sherry, a 25-year-old mother of three, explains: "*My house was shot up. There was a lot of drug activity there, but this happened out of blue. I left one morning with my kids to go to a girlfriend's house. While we were at her house, someone decided to rob my neighbor. They broke in the door, came through my house to get up there, raped my upstairs neighbor's girlfriend, and shot at her, but they missed. . . . And my neighbor came home through the back door during this time and the guys ran down and they started shooting back and forth and they shot up my house. . . . I went to my sister's house and stayed there for a day, but it was too small, and then the next day at my girlfriend's. And then I called crisis services and they suggested to call here.*"

Heather, a 27-year-old single mother of four boys ages 2 to 11 years, said: "*I hurt my knee and had to have a brace on my leg and went to stay*

*with my sister for a month. . . . And the [neighbor]hood is all drug infested
and they [drug users] broke into my house. They stole my refrigerator,
water pipes, and heater, and gutted the place. The pipes and heaters sell
good on the streets. The whole place got all flooded, and all my stuff was
water logged. I had a lot of wood [furniture], and there's nothing I can
salvage, not much. They got in through the window that my landlady took
out. But she claimed that it wasn't her fault and was dragging on giving
me the papers [title to the house]; I was leasing the house to own. She
said I owed her back rent and this and that. I couldn't stay at the place
anyway, so I went and stayed with my sister."*

Lynn, a 31-year-old mother of two young children, said: *"I had to
get up and leave because my husband was being abusive. And then the
neighborhood was filled with drug dealers. It was a little street, and the
drug dealers didn't want me there because I didn't fit in with them. I was
in their way. So, just before the Fourth of July, they tried to jump me when
I was coming home with the groceries. I was pregnant. And my husband,
he had just got high and he had spent up most of our public assistance
grant on some crack. He had just started taking crack."*

Ellen, a 32-year-old single mother of four boys ages 13, 11, 10, and 9
years, said that, in the face of drug-related violence, the police did not
help the victims but victimized them even more: *"A friend of my cousin's
lived next door to me. He came over to my home and threatened to break
into my home and rape me in front of my boys. I called the police, but the
police took forever, over 2 hours, to come. And they [the police] ended
up beating up my boyfriend, two of my cousins, and a friend really bad."*

Drug Use of Family Members and Roommates

Immediate family members or roommates of the interviewed parents
were also often using drugs, and the parents were not only running
from the neighborhood but from their own families and roommates.
Gina, a 32-year-old mother of two teenagers, said: *"I walked away from
everything, my job, my husband. I was just tired. I was working. I was
working full time. But it was drugs, and it wasn't me; it was him."* Donna,
a 39-year-old mother of five children ages 7 through 14, said that her
husband sold everything in the house, including the children's clothes,
to satisfy his drug habit and had sexually abused her for 3 days when
she and the children finally decided to seek shelter.

Erica, a 19-year-old mother of two children under age 2 who had
another on the way, said: *"It was a whole house, five bedrooms, basement,
really big, but I had to leave. I had a roommate, and I came home one*

day and everything in my house was gone. Come to find out she was using drugs or whatever. I didn't know that. Her room was upstairs; mine was downstairs. There was paraphernalia up there. I went to my mother's. She was using drugs too. I couldn't take it—it's, like, everywhere. It's bad for my kids because then [when she's on drugs] she's like a totally different person." As in the case of Michael, whom we described earlier, Erica did not receive support from her family when she needed it because of the family members' drug problems. Erica added: "*A friend of mine said it's easier to get your Section 8 if you're here, and if you don't have the [drug] problems, they help you find a house.*"

Battered Women

For about half of the women who listed domestic violence as the primary reason for their homelessness, this was the first such homeless episode. For the other half, however, there had been at least one previous stop at a homeless shelter for the same reason. Many women who listed the reason for the current episode of homelessness as something other than domestic violence also indicated that they had been homeless once or twice before because of domestic violence. A significant proportion of the homeless mothers had been in an abusive relationship, sometimes more than once. They had seen and experienced violence within and without and had lived constantly in fear. Jan, a 34-year-old mother of four young children with another on the way and a domestic violence victim, told us that her sister had been killed by a man with whom she was in an abusive relationship about a year earlier. Her sister's killing increased Jan's fear for her own safety and led her to a shelter at that time, but she had gone back to the same environment until she had returned to the shelter this time. The emotional scars also ran deeper among domestic violence victims. Elaine, a 25-year-old mother of 6- and 7-year-old boys, told us about the effect of her estranged boyfriend's attempt to rape her and shooting at her in front of her two boys: "*The cops brought me straight here. I'm from this area, but I don't trust nobody right now. . . .* "

Disability due to violence was common. Cindy, a 23-year-old mother of two young children, said: "*I have been a home health aide for the last 2 years, but I'm on disability now. I couldn't go back to school [she was a sophomore in college] either, because I couldn't take the exams because of what happened to me.*"

Nevertheless, we saw a distinctive difference between the attitudes of women who came to a shelter because of domestic violence and the attitudes of the rest of the women. The former usually stated: "*I did not lose it [housing]. It [coming to a shelter] was my choice.*" Freedom from imminent danger and fear of physical abuse also gave these women and their children a sense of relief, although shelter life, of course, was not an ideal alternative.

Frances, a 32-year-old mother of two school-age children, said: "*The cops wouldn't take his keys away because he's my husband. Nobody ever hit me if we couldn't get along. . . . Everything was always wrong. . . . He'd say I was nothing. . . . Once we married he was different. I never knew what was going to happen. I never told nobody about it. We'd go to church together like the perfect family, and then we'd get home and it was all different. If I were to call one of my friends, they wouldn't believe it. It would be like, 'What's the matter with you?' He would go after the kids. When they were left with him, they couldn't relax and do what kids should be able to do. . . . I was working and then he wouldn't show up at home and he'd spend the money, and I went on public assistance because I couldn't get to work because I'd have to get the kids to school. I said I'd leave, but then I stayed. Leaving was the best thing I ever did. I don't want to be somebody's accidental death. The kids needed a place where they can come in and relax and a mom that can smile. The only reason I stuck around was because he was my husband, I thought I should stay. Here I am starting all over again. I believe in God. I'm doing my part, and I know God didn't put me here for no one to beat me. I praise the Lord, and he's given me strength. I am gonna get what I can and move on—my kids' beds and sentimental things. . . . I am gonna get an order of protection and move on. I am gonna get my GED [high school equivalency diploma] because I dropped out of school. I owe it to my mother, my kids, and myself. Start all over. I try and tell younger kids, my nieces and nephews, 'Don't you dare drop out of school.'* " Frances had a lot on her mind, and she talked to us for over 3 1/2 hours straight.

Vicky, a 34-year-old mother of two children, 7 and 4 years old, told us how she ended up coming to a shelter in the city from her house and her lower-middle-class life in a small town: "*Yeah, right, I left him [her husband] twice other than this, I left him twice, once for 6 months and once for 4 months. . . . The first time was on May 18, 1992; I had to come to a shelter because he was violent and disciplinary to my daughter [1 year old then]. He hit her in the mouth. My husband was possessive: He used to prevent me from driving my car; he used to throw my car keys out the window. I wouldn't even be able to make it to the kids' doctor unless I found myself a ride. . . . Yeah, yeah, I can definitely see good*

*changes in [her son]. I can see when he's here he's not as violent with his
sister as he used to be. He still is, but not as bad. He was constantly,
constantly touching his sister in a violent way, hitting and pulling her,
nudging her, or pushing constantly. He has seen too much that his father
has done, and I believe he himself thought that's the right way to handle
situations. His junior kindergarten teacher saw things out of him. I told my
husband that this teacher was seeing things out of him. He [her husband]
kind of stopped his violence in the house for a while, not a long time, and
[the child] became a whole different person. His teacher saw it, his father
saw it, and I saw it. Then pressures would start on my husband, and that's
when all the violence would start all over again. And then [the child] would
start being violent again. The teachers knew our problem and always said,
'Get out of it,' and I was just too dumbfounded to do it. . . . Now, nothing's
going to prevent me from finding a place. I've just got to start my life all
over again. It's just a stopping point in my life, and everything's sorted out
for my children and myself."*

Margaret, a 34-year-old mother of three, ages 14, 12, and 3, also left
her house in a small town near Syracuse to come to the shelter. She
and her children were initially placed in a different shelter but decided
to move to the current shelter because Margaret was afraid that her
boyfriend might be able to find them. The children were having a hard
time adjusting to shelter life: "*[The third child's] father was threatening
to kill me. I figured I'd better get far away just in case. So we went to
downtown to a domestic violence office, and they helped us. My older girls
told me that I should have just killed him so they [the children] could have
stayed at home.*"

Maria is a 36-year-old mother of nine children; the oldest two (19 and
18 years old) are married and live independently, five others live with
her ex-husband in New York City, and the two youngest (ages 1 year
and 4 months), the product of her liaison with her 25-year-old boyfriend,
are with her. She left the boyfriend, the father of the two youngest
children, "*after so many months of abuse, I mean, years and months of
abuse.*" Five years ago Maria had another episode of shelter living with
her seven older children for the same reason (involving her then-hus-
band) and told us about the difficulty with the two oldest's "*delinquent
behavior that got worse*" in the shelter. She, like most mothers in a
similar situation, also told us of her children's emotional and academic
problems that she thought might have something to do with the violence
at home. Understandably, the adolescents had a harder time adjusting
to shelter life than did the younger children, and those who were exposed to domestic violence appeared to have even more difficulty.

CAREGIVER MOVERS

Although not many of the families were in the "caregiver movers" category, the circumstances under which they ended up in homeless shelters were entirely different from those of the other families. Terri, a 35-year-old mother of four children ages 18 through 13, had come to Buffalo from Pennsylvania to take care of her sick mother: "*We went to my mom's, but we couldn't stay. She lives in a [public housing] project, and my son can stay, but with all of us, she could get kicked out. It was like someone was watching there and I didn't want her to get kicked out. So we came to the shelter.*" In Pennsylvania, Terri had been on public assistance and had also worked as a cleaner; she was in the process of applying for New York State public assistance benefits.

Louise, a 26-year-old mother of three children ages 8 through 1 years, told us a similar story regarding her long-distance move and ensuing residency in a homeless shelter: "*My mom lives here and she got sick, and it was too hard and expensive coming back and forth, so we came here. We lived here [in the town] before, but originally we're from [a nearby town]. My mom is having a lot of health problems; she gets dialysis four times a week. . . . We stayed with my mom for two nights, but she only has a one-bedroom in public housing, and it was crowded and she could have been kicked out because of us. I have a few relatives, but they can't really help; I mean, they have their own kids and there's no space anywhere.*" Louise was on public assistance. In the past, she had worked as a nurse's assistant, and she said she wanted to get recertified in New York State.

For both Terri and Louise, it appeared that their move was somewhat voluntary and that it did not affect their life as much, at least in an economic sense. Both had had a tough time managing a not-so-small family on their welfare benefits, and their housing status had not been entirely stable: Louise had been homeless once before she moved.

Unlike these two, Lisa's move from North Carolina was more involuntary than voluntary, because both she and her fiancé had good semi-skilled jobs there ("*making good money*") and she regrets it now: "*I was born in Buffalo. The majority of my family is here. My mother was sick and begged me to move back to Buffalo. I had a good job down there [in North Carolina]. It took me 2 months to decide to come. My fiancé [and her two children] came up with me. When I got up here, things didn't work out like we had talked about over the phone. She [her mother] had a boyfriend. The house was crowded. There were too many people in the house. We didn't disagree or anything, but I went to stay with my sister. She lives in the same apartments. I was at my mom's for two days and my sister's a week or some days.*" At the time of her interview, Lisa and her fiancé were looking for jobs in Buffalo. Because of their educational background (2 years of college) and skills, they were not expecting much difficulty finding jobs. Nevertheless, Lisa said: "*[The move] set me back.*"

LONG-DISTANCE MOVERS AND MANY-TIMES MOVERS

We found that some of these families had been long-distance movers in search of work opportunities and/or social support. Some had moved to several states in a futile search for a better life. Others had moved from one place to another without a clear purpose, and they eventually ended up in a shelter or were moving from one shelter to another.

Beverly, a 37-year-old mother of a 10-year-old (and a 20-year-old who lives elsewhere), said: "*My girlfriend, I met her down South and she went to Buffalo and she told me it was nice in Buffalo. See, when I was down South, I was only working a temporary job, so I had nothing to lose. She said I could come up to Buffalo, they had jobs and I could stay with her a couple of months until I can get a job and get my own place. Meanwhile, when I was staying there, she and her friends were doing drugs, and I didn't want me and my baby in that situation. I don't have any family here. So that's when I called the shelter, and they told me I could come.*" Owing to her previous work history, Beverly was able to find a couple of temporary jobs as soon as she moved. She told us that she had saved some money while she was working and that she relies on it when she is out of work.

Bonnie, a 30-year-old mother of two children, 10 and 7 years old, said: "*I moved to Little Rock, Arkansas, and then 3 months later I came back because I had to come and get the children, and the relationship I was in, I just wanted to leave it alone. When I came back, I had no place to stay. Well, I stayed with the kids' grandmother for a month. The kids were at their dad's mother's while I was in Arkansas, and when I came back I didn't know their father had moved in too. We got into arguments. And his mother was telling everybody in the house to get out by the first of the year. Well, I decided to just leave rather than put up with the problems and listen to it all the time.*"

Cheryl, a 39-year-old mother of three children ages 6, 5, and 2 years, had become homeless in Ohio 16 months earlier and had stayed in two different shelters there: "*I was going through changes with my boyfriend. I just wanted to get away from him for a while and think about things. . . . Then I got sick and [her daughter] got sick, so we came up here in March and just decided to stay. When we first came here, we stayed with my sister. I moved out from there to here because we could get things [public housing application] done quicker. . . . I have a drinking problem and they drink down there, and I didn't want to get back into that. That's how I became homeless in the first place, you know?"* In the meantime, Cheryl had found a new boyfriend, and he was staying with them at the shelter where we interviewed her. He had recently found a part-time housekeeping job at a social services agency.

Virginia, a 33-year-old mother of an 11- and a 10-year-old, had moved back and forth between New York and two other states and had just come back to New York when we interviewed her. She had moved out twice to different states because of marriages. Both marriages had ended in divorce (due to domestic violence), and she had returned to her hometown each time. Before her recent return, she had stayed in a shelter in another state. The children from her first marriage had been taken from her 10 years earlier, and she had recently been able to regain custody of them. At the time we interviewed her, she had found a job as a cashier and hoped to settle down this time.

Roseanne, a 20-year-old mother of two young children, had moved back and forth between New York and California: *"I'm from Buffalo. My stepfather was in the military, and he got stationed in [a city in California] and we were there for 13 years and then we came here—a whole bunch of family. I went back to California and rented an apartment from my aunt. And then I came to Buffalo in 1993, and I left back to [a city in California] February this year, and then when I came back in July, I was homeless. . . . In California, we lived in the baby's uncle's house, and he was trying to have sex with me. I wouldn't and he kicked us out. I went to the baby's aunt's house, and we moved from there because we were having problems at her house. And we came back to Buffalo."* Roseanne has no work experience and receives no real support from any relatives. (*"Well, it's just me taking care of my kids. I don't have any help. The fathers [of her children] . . . huh, joke."*) It appeared that her interstate moves had been motivated by her search for social and financial—including housing—support from other people, but none of the moves resulted in any positive gains. Roseanne told us that she is planning to enroll in a community college, get off welfare, and find a job. As a high school dropout, she has a long way to go to be able to put that plan to work.

Danielle, a 23-year-old mother of a 5-year-old (and a 4-year-old, who is in the custody of her father), had made interstate moves and had been chronically homeless. Most recently, she worked for 2 months in Oregon. When she was laid off, she lost her apartment; she and her 5-year-old lived by moving back and forth between her grandmothers:

"[One grandma] would keep him and I'd go to the other grandma, and I'd switch for the week or something." After 2 months of switching back and forth between grandmothers, they moved to New York and stayed at *"my stepmom's and a friend's and a relative of his father's."* Like Roseanne, Danielle had never been to a homeless shelter, but, again like Roseanne, she had never really had her own place. She told us that she had moved *"15, maybe 20 times"* in the previous 2 years. The frequent moves led to her son's missing school (kindergarten) for months. Danielle told us that she could not find an apartment of her own because *"the rent is basically the entire amount that PA gives me."*

Another group that had been frequently on the move without purpose were those who had self-identified substance abuse problems. In the process of our interviews, we also came to suspect mental health problems among many of these people. Although we did not utilize any clinical assessment or diagnostic tools, based on clinical social work training and experience, we suspected that mental health issues were at hand for many of these homeless families. When we interviewed Lois, 34 years old, and her husband, Jim, 38 years old, they had seven children with them at the shelter, five of their own and two of Lois's sister's. Two of the couple's other children, as well as Lois's sister, were being incarcerated. The couple, originally from Buffalo, had moved to another state 3 years earlier, had used drugs, and had moved about four or five times in the preceding 2 years alone. Most recently (3 months earlier), they had stayed in a homeless shelter in another state, but they decided to move to another shelter in Buffalo, where we interviewed them. The reason for the move was not obvious; they clearly stated that they were not looking for work. Both Lois and Jim showed signs not only of drug abuse but of mental health problems as well.

SUMMARY

These parents' description of the circumstances under which they became homeless reveals the nonexistence or tenuousness of a safety net that would have guaranteed even the most basic necessity of their lives—a shelter for them and their children. Because most of them had been living with a bare minimum level of economic resources, they were literally one paycheck or welfare check away from homelessness. When a welfare or Social Security check did not arrive in their mailboxes, they had no other recourse, no alternative line of defense against losing their homes. When they no longer had their meager paycheck in their hands, homelessness became an immediate reality. Even with these checks, their economic situations were so precarious that many of them were, as described by a parent, only "$15.00" away from losing their apartments. Thus the threat of becoming homeless must have been looming large for many of the interviewed parents in their daily struggle to keep the household economics together; and the loss of their homes was like falling from the end of a rope onto which they had been trying to hang tightly.

On top of the lack of an economic safety net, these parents' stories also reveal an absence of a formal human services network to which they could have turned to prevent their becoming homeless. Parents who were preyed upon by unscrupulous landlords and/or faced illegal eviction had no easy recourse to redress the situation. Their complaints against the landlords were met by unsympathetic and unresponsive bureaucracies, including the law enforcement system. Despite the fact that many parents and children faced constant threats from violence and crime in their neighborhoods, they did not have access to any services that could have helped them find safe housing before they fell victims to violence and crime and became homeless. Most of the interviewed parents had not been connected to a human services system, and thus were devoid of any coping resources both before and after the crisis of victimization and homelessness hit them. The parents, even those with substance abuse and other mental health problems, were on their own. If the families had had access to adequate preventive services, many would have been able to avoid homelessness and its devastating physical and psychological consequences.

4

Short Stops: Living Doubled Up

As described in chapter 3, a majority of these families did not come to a shelter directly after they lost their homes, but had gone to stay with a relative and/or friend. We were amazed by the generosity of some relatives (mostly parents and/or siblings) who provided food and shelter for their homeless children, grandchildren, and/or siblings for months. In almost all cases, however, living doubled up lasted for only a short period, ranging from a night or two to a week or two, mostly because the relatives and friends did not have enough space and other resources to accommodate the homeless families. Most homeless families reported that the relative's and/or friend's house became too crowded for them to stay there any longer. The spatial problems also caused much stress among the family members, creating tensions or worsening existing ones in their relationship with the host while they lived doubled up. The stress and the sour relationship between host and homeless family frequently drove the latter to a shelter. Others told us that the public housing projects or private rental units where their relatives live prohibit such doubled-up living arrangements. Several parents also told us that they had had to leave the relative's or a friend's house because the host person/family used drugs or engaged in other lifestyles that they could not approve of and that they feared could have negative effects on their children.

For almost all of the families who had lived doubled up with a relative or friend before entering a shelter, that relative or friend was their only social support system. A majority of the homeless parents we interviewed did not hesitate to tell us that they had a very tenuous or no social support system for the following reasons: (1) Their relatives or friends, whose economic situations are often only a little better than theirs, were not able to spare anything more than some "advice." (2) The homeless parents' relationship with their relatives had not been very close due to preexisting disputes and problems. (3) The homeless parents did not want to burden their relatives or friends or they were too ashamed to tell them about the homelessness. (4) The relatives or friends had substance abuse, relationship, or other lifestyle problems that they did not approve of.

Homeless families also frequently told us that they chose a shelter over a relative's or friend's house because shelters provide home-finding services; connect them to other necessary services, such as public assistance, job training, and counseling; and give them, especially domestic violence victims, top priority status on waiting lists for public housing or Section 8 vouchers. We found that some families who lived in substandard housing while waiting for a public housing or Section 8 voucher for years had consciously left their housing to come to a shelter, so that they would be able to make the short list.

In this chapter we quote the homeless parents' comments about the stress of living doubled up and the extent and their perceptions of social support.

STRESS OF LIVING DOUBLED UP

Crowding and Stress

Marie, Terri, and Louise had all stayed with their mothers in one-bedroom apartments in public housing projects. Stress built up not only because of crowding but also because of a fear that their mothers might be evicted for having unauthorized overnight guests. Marie said: "*We were staying with my mother, and my mother lives in a one-bedroom apartment and . . . because she is on SSI [Supplemental Security Income], they really don't allow children to be there. So she was in a very stressful situation, and I think we all were because there were three adults [the mother, Marie, and her husband], and my sister and her child were living with us too. I was getting very much depressed and stressed out, and my* husband was already depressed because of the failure of his job. You know, he was still working, but it just wasn't what he needed for his family. So as he was in a stressful situation, I think our relationship or communication started to lack. So he went to stay with his sister, and I just got fed up. . . . I was always hollering at my children, maybe tossing them about, and hitting them. And I'm not that type of person and I knew it was getting to me. And I knew I wasn't myself, because I was excessively eating and I just really became very much depressed."

Terri said: "She [her mother] lives in a project and my son can stay, but with all of us, she could get kicked out. It was like someone was watching there and I didn't want her to get kicked out. . . . I have two brothers, but we're having family disputes." Louise said the same thing: "We stayed with my mom for 2 nights, but she only has a one-bedroom in public housing, and it was crowded and she could have been kicked out because of us. . . . I have a few relatives, but they can't really help; I mean, they have their own kids and there's no space anywhere."

Others described the crowding in a relative's or a friend's house, often because the hosts had three or four children of their own and the homeless family, with three or four children, would join them in a two-bedroom apartment. After her apartment was shot up, Sherry and her three children went to stay at her sister's and a friend's place for only a day each because the apartments were too small for so many children from two families. She also said that it was very uncomfortable to live in someone else's home. Brenda told us: "I [and her six children] first stayed with my brother-in-law. My sister had died, and my brother-in-law was a bachelor. He had a one-bedroom. There just was not a lot of room. He had company coming over, and kids were sleeping on the floor." Brenda and her family had been invited by an elderly woman friend to move to Buffalo from Virginia and stay with her for a rent of $200. However, both the host and the guest soon found that "living with six kids is too much"; furthermore, Brenda felt that the elderly friend was verbally and emotionally abusive to her children. According to Brenda, the children were "cursed at and scared to use the bathroom without getting yelled at." That was why Brenda came to the shelter, and she said that her children "feel more comfortable here." Brenda told us that she was not close to her family because she grew up in foster care.

Disputes often erupted in the doubled-up arrangements, driving families to the shelters. Virginia stayed at her mother's for 3 months and described their disputes that led her and her children to a shelter: "My mother decided that if I wasn't going to live by her rules, I needed to find another place to stay. She didn't want me to work, she wanted me to stay *home with the kids, and she basically wanted to control my and my kids' lives, and I wouldn't allow her to do so."*

Lisa also told us that her family had to leave her mother's house after 2 nights, because "*the house was crowded*" with too many people there. Then she went to stay with her sister, who lived in the same apartment complex. She told us that for a week and some days her family stayed at her sister's: "*My sister would tell my mother stuff about me; then my mother would call me to see what was going on. I told her that I didn't have any idea. She would tell me that my sister wants me out. Why didn't she [sister] tell me that? We are grown women. I am not about to kiss up to anyone. I've been on my own since I was 14 practically. I get this real quick—shelter life.*"

Chris told us that, following their eviction, she and her children had stayed at a motel for a couple of weeks, and that they had then gone to the home of her brother, her only family connection, but had ended up back at a motel: "*We had a big argument. His daughter was getting away with a lot of stuff, and I couldn't take it no more. There were seven of us all together. . . . No, no other family, and our friends have too many in their apartments too.*"

Before they came to the shelter, Jan, a domestic violence victim, and her four children had gone to live with a couple of different friends: "*I got tired of it, going from house to house. Also, I was getting uncomfortable. Everybody got their own problems that they deal with. I had to deal with my stuff, and theirs was on top of it. So I came here because I figured I could deal with my own stuff here. I even signed up for a psychiatric evaluation on my own. I got a lot of pain to get out.*"

Drug Use by the Host and Other Problems

Some homeless families who had gone to stay with relatives found themselves in even worse chaos, because the relatives often "*don't live correctly themselves.*" Jessica said: "*I left my aunt's house because I found drugs around the house. My aunt smoked crack. This was when I just started to get my money from SSI [Supplemental Security Income], and she kept asking me for money even though I was paying rent to stay there. I would say no, and she would get mad. I was paying rent and didn't even have my own room, and she had nine other people living there. It was crowded. And she kept talking about me and hurting my feelings—that I'm stupid and I don't deserve my child. I just couldn't take it anymore. I told my social worker and she talked to her about it and then my aunt got mad, saying, 'Why are you telling those people what I told you?' I told her that's because I'm sensitive, and then she said, 'Get out.'*"

Other homeless parents had faced similar situations in a relative's or a friend's household and had had to leave because they were worried about its negative effects on their children. Noreen decided to come to the shelter from her aunt's house: *"I was staying with an aunt of mine, but it wasn't the kind of place I wanted to stay. They do things I don't do, so I had to leave. . . . I'm not into drugs, and different people in the family do that and I don't care for that. I want to better myself. With my aunt, even though she didn't do it in front of the kids, it still was. . . . "* Georgia and Doug, recovering alcoholics who *"just got out of rehab,"* went to stay with a friend, but *"there was too much drinking and drugs going on there."* Rosemary, a 47-year-old mother of a 15-year-old daughter who often ran away from home, initially stayed at her older daughter's house. She had to leave, though, because of *"the company she [the older daughter] was keeping—got men all over,"* as well as the landlord's discovery of Rosemary and her younger daughter as unauthorized guests of the house.

Unwilling or Distant Relatives

Some homeless families' plea for temporary lodging were turned down by their relatives. Debby said: *"I went to my son's aunt's house, and I asked her if I could stay there until I get my next check to pay on the apartment. And she told me that somebody had broken into her house and she didn't want no trouble and that she didn't want nothing like that to happen again. She wasn't saying that she didn't trust me; she just didn't feel comfortable because of what just happened to her."*

Others told us about their discomfort at staying at a relative's house because of preexisting problems. Jennifer said: *"I stayed with my family for 4 days, which was as long as I could. I am not real close with them, so it was awkward."* Fred said: *"My sister wants me to move in with her to [their father's house]. And that's gonna be kind of hard for me to do. I was raised in that house. My dad used to beat my mom in that house, and she passed away in that house. I don't want to go back there. Nine out of 10, my dad is gonna die in that house, probably in a couple of more weeks. But I don't think I really want to go back there. A lot of memories. . . . Moreover, drugs and stuff around on [the street where the house is located] is really, really bad."*

EXTENT AND PERCEPTIONS OF SOCIAL SUPPORT

Most of the interviewed parents were well aware that they were by themselves when it came to the extent of informal social support. As just described, their relatives and/or friends tended to be in a similar economic/housing predicament, and they often had other problems to deal with. Mothers and sisters were major sources of social support for many homeless parents. Others, however, told us that their mothers were dead or that they were not close to their fathers or that they did not get along with the rest of their family of origin. For single mothers, ex-husbands or ex-partners who helped out were a rarity. Also, although many homeless parents expressed their faith in God, only two listed church members as sources of social support. In the following section we tried to describe the extent of homeless families' social support.

Mothers and Sisters

In most cases, mothers and sisters tried to help the homeless parents and their children to the best of their abilities. For example, a grand-mother was the most frequently mentioned custodian of the children who had not accompanied their mothers to a shelter. Grandmothers were apparently trying to help the family by taking care of one or more children even though they were not able to help the entire family in its time of hardship. By keeping the children at home, grandmothers tried to shield them from the potentially chaotic life at a shelter, to ensure that they finished the school year at the same school, and to free up some of the mothers' time so they could find housing. One grandmother bought bus tokens for her teenage grandson so that even while he was staying at the shelter, he could attend the same school. Grandmothers also helped their homeless grandchildren by providing an occasional sanctuary from the shelter life. Several families told us that they regu-larly went over to "*Grandma's house*" for lunch, play, movies, or some-thing that "*would help children to take their minds off the situation that they are in.*"

Sisters were another frequently mentioned source of social support for many homeless parents. They often provided temporary boarding to homeless parents and their children, and they were also frequently the ones who provided them with information on the shelters. Sisters did not keep their homeless nieces and nephews in their houses as much as the children's grandmothers did, but they, like the latter, provided occasional home-cooked meals and other types of relief from shelter life.

Other Relatives

Besides mothers and sisters, only a few homeless parents mentioned other relatives—the children's fathers, cousins, sisters-in-law, a few friends—as their sources of social support. After grandmothers, the children's fathers were the most frequently mentioned custodians of children who did not accompany their mothers to a shelter. Beyond custody, however, the fathers did not help much. One mother explained that her children's father used to provide "*occasional baby-sitting.*" Another told us that her children's father, who lived in Indiana, "*helps when he can,*" and yet another told us that her children's fathers were "*a joke.*"

Tammy had given up the custody of her 15-year-old to his father a long time ago, and she was never awarded child support for her youngest daughter "*because he [the father] is in prison so the judge said he wouldn't be able to pay.*" For her two middle children, ages 8 and 9, however, she said: "*Their dad was court ordered to pay $264.50 a month for the two of them, and he doesn't pay a thing. He is an eye doctor and makes over $170,000 a year. I know where he is [in a different state], and I told everybody. I've got his home phone number, his work address, and ain't nobody doing nothing to help me. He owes me, like, $35,000 in child support. It makes me so angry because here he owns a house, has two cars, he's got a new baby, and . . . they live like a king and a queen, and I'm fighting just to make it.*"

Cousins, sisters-in-law, and friends provided homeless families boarding for periods and storage places for their belongings; they also connected them to homeless shelters, although they did that much less frequently than sisters. Only a few homeless parents mentioned their fathers as sources of social support. In cases in which both parents were alive and married to each other, the homeless parents tended to describe their fathers as supportive. They seldom described their widowed fathers as supportive, however, and in fact generally perceived their relationships with their fathers as conflict ridden and hostile. Other homeless parents told us that they had not had much contact with their fathers. Like fathers, brothers were seldom a source of support. Many homeless parents mentioned strained relationships between themselves and their brothers. A few middle-aged homeless parents had older children who lived independently. These children, also often dependent on public assistance, were in no way able to help their homeless parents. In the case of David, he was so ashamed of his homelessness that he was hiding it from his relatives, including his older daughter, who lived in a neighborhood not far from the shelter. To our query as to whether he had any social support, David answered: "*Yes, yes. But I don't know how to tell them and be accepted for pride on my part. I thank God for the [shelter]. If I can help in any way, I will do it. I have done some volunteering.*"

No Social Support

When asked about their social support, a large proportion of homeless parents indicated that they did not have any. Some, like Beverly and Hilary, who moved from other parts of the country in search of a better life, literally did not have any relatives or friends they would be able to turn to. Hilary said: "*I have no family at all whatsoever. My family is either in New York, Puerto Rico, or Florida. I came here so they [her children] could have a better life, not so wild like in New York City.*" Others flatly told us that they did not even talk to their family. Still others, like Mary, had very tenuous social support networks that they had to be careful not to overburden. Mary answered our question as to whether she had any social support: "*Yes, but not really. [Since her mother died] I have just one person, but I don't want to overdo it. So I just kind of maintain myself.*" Others indicated that they had relatives but no support. Rosemary said: "*Most of my family is here except for my son, who just got married in [another city]. Even though I know people here, it's not like I got anybody. You know, my mom is here too, but she's got foster kids who are my nieces and nephews who my sister abandoned. She got her hands full, and I just couldn't lay it all on her.*" Louise also said that, in addition to her mother, who lived in a one-bedroom apartment in a public housing project, "*I have a few relatives, but they really can't help. I mean, they have their own kids, and there's no space anywhere.*" Amanda, who had lived with a sister some years earlier, when she became homeless for the first time, said: "*I'm the youngest of 10 kids, so they [her siblings] can be my support, but I chose not to overburden them. They have already done so much because they think of me as the baby, and I'm not going to constantly keep them in my business.*" When Sherry said the following, it appeared that she spoke for the majority of homeless parents: "*Well, it's like I was telling [the director of the shelter], it's me. My support, emotional support and encouragement, I'm by myself, mostly me and God.*"

5

At the Shelter

Life at a congregate shelter can be a challenge even in the best of circumstances. There are institutional rules the families are required to abide by, and those who break the rules will be given penalties (blue slip, pink slips, points) that could result in their eviction from the shelter. Most shelters are run on a shoestring budget, and the underpaid, overworked staff may not always have the time and energy to be sensitive to each family's diverse needs and provide adequate assistance for them. New families are always coming in and old families are leaving. Shared living space, congregate dining, interaction with so many people, and the lack of privacy often create a sense of chaos and lead many parents to feel completely out of structure. In these circumstances, some children frequently act out and others become withdrawn and cling to their parents. Older children also invariably have to deal with a sense of shame and fear that their classmates and teachers may discover they are homeless. The parents grieve for the loss of their own home, freedom, peace, and control over their lives and their children, and they frequently engage in self-blaming for their homeless situation. They also experience humiliation and indignity from disrespectful treatment by shelter staff and DSS caseworkers. At the same time, many feel grateful for the safety of and services available at a shelter. Indeed for many families, the only alternative to the shelter is the streets, which would surely tear the children from the parents and push the families down into an abyss of sheer misery.

In this chapter, we examine the recurring themes regarding the parents' experience of homelessness at shelters and their perception of the psychosocial and health-related problems of their children. The chapter begins with the presentation of the parents' fear and relief at the doorstep of a shelter, then proceeds to their experience of shelter life and dealings with housing and welfare bureaucracies.

FEAR AND RELIEF

As shown in chapter 3, before coming to a shelter, most of the parents interviewed had lived in extreme poverty in inner-city neighborhoods infested with drugs and violence. Their lives had already been compromised by harsh living conditions in substandard housing and unsafe neighborhoods, as well as by the vagaries of the welfare bureaucracy and flimsiness of minimum-wage jobs. Consequently, they experienced potential, if not real, instability and uncertainty about the future. Still, when they came into the shelter, they were crushed by the loss of their home and terrified of the unknowns of shelter life.

Cathy: "*It's a new experience, right. Yeah, I cried when I first came. I was scared. I said, 'Oh, my goodness.'* "

Erica: "*This is my first time. I was scared to come in here. One big room with a bunch of winos and drug addicts.*"

Michelle: "*You never think it will happen, but it does.*"

Tammy: "*When we got ready to come here, I was in tears. I didn't want to come here. I was scared to death, and I know that had an impact on [her daughter].*"

They were also relieved and grateful for the shelter and the assistance. As discussed earlier, some had come to the shelter with some knowledge of the services available there. Even if they had not known it before, many came to realize that the shelter opened doors to a variety of community resources and that they could take advantage of many in-house programs, such as day care and different kinds of workshops there. In addition, mothers who had fled domestic violence perceived the shelter as a refuge and a sort of halfway house between their past and the next phase of their lives.

Betty: "*I am just glad that they had something like this available, because it's needed. It's needed. You never know when you're going to be out in the streets, so it's good to know you can go somewhere.*"

Andrea: "*Here they're helpful for me and the kids. This facility is great. It's nice that they have a place for people that are homeless to come and regain themselves. If we weren't here, we'd be out in the snow or cold. I am just happy to be here now."*

Tammy: *"[But for the shelter] they [her children] would have ended up homeless and maybe dead. I think about that, I am so lucky to be here. I know my kids have a roof over their heads. It may not be the best meals, but they've got a place and I don't have to worry about them getting hurt. They are my life and if anything ever happened to them, I would be devastated."*

Marian: *"They could have some better food in here. But I'm, I mean, I'm homeless. I get no assistance, so I can't go out and get me anything else. . . . Being a homeless individual, it's not so bad living here and I'll thank whoever I need to. It's not the worst place. It's a place where you can get three meals, wash your clothes, and rest your head. I am thankful for that."*

Sandy: *"When I first came here . . . I had such an attitude, like somebody here owes me something. Then I started to realize: When you're here, you're lucky. You have a roof over your head and my family is together, and I started to be a little more grateful."*

Terri: *"Before we came here, I was a nervous wreck. I was crying the whole way down here. I didn't want to, but my kids, well, I had to bring them here. I have a saying, where I go they go and where they go, I go. So we came and this gave us an address to get a case [PA] opened. Homeless people should know there are places to go to and they are not so bad. It's someplace I can call home; this is home for now."*

CHALLENGES OF SHELTER LIVING

Grief and Guilt

Relief and gratitude aside, life at a shelter was the antithesis to stability and privacy, as indicated by a strong yearning for "peace of mind," a phrase that one parent after another used to describe his or her longings for a home. Grieving for a lost home lingered. Although the homes they had left were usually uninhabitable places, the parents who were interviewed grieved for the loss of a sense of independence and privacy. Separated from children and other family members, life at a shelter can be also very isolating and disconnected, and depression about the situation was common.

Annette: *"Life is hectic here. You are surrounded by strangers. [At home] I guess we'd have a lot more peace, peace of mind, time. And then you're afraid to bring clothes and stuff like that because of it getting stolen."*

Marie: "*There was a structure when I left home; there was a set time for my children to play with toys. There's not a whole lot of TV in my home. But I'm totally out of structure here, because you got people telling you what to do to your own children, you know, and I don't mind especially if someone's much older than I. People order you around here. It feels like I got cameras all around me. . . . If we're in Mass or we're in chapel, they tell me, 'Let your children sit with the other kids.' If we were to go to a church [back at home], we always sat as a family.*"

Angela: "*I just take it one day at a time because I try not to cry so much.*"

Marian: "*My mom's in the hospital and I can't get to see her 'cause I don't have a car or anything.*"

Sandy: "*Everything is coming down at once. We have been together for 7 years before we got married and been married 13 years coming Monday, and we have three kids and they miss their daddy because he's not here. They are going through something, but I am too. We are a very close family and it's hard. I cry too sometimes. I feel very depressed.*"

Jacqueline: "*You know, you got new people coming in, old people leaving, and kids running around, roughhousing and stuff, a lot of noise and a lot of commotion for him [her baby]. . . . It gets frustrating. . . .*"

Parents' self-blaming for their homelessness and their guilt toward and sadness for their children were also very common, even when the circumstances under which they had become homeless were beyond their control. For example, Cathy had had to leave her rental unit because her landlord had informed her that the house was being sold and that the new landlord was asking much higher rent. She found out later that the landlord had lied to her about the sale of the house; he had gotten rid of her to be able to lease the unit to another family for a higher rent. Cathy and her two daughters had lived at her mother's house for 2 months before they came to the shelter, at the advice of a friend, in the hope of finding a house of their own. Cathy was very depressed when we interviewed her and blamed herself for the situation: "*I cry for my daughter. She goes, 'Mommy, what's the matter?' and I say, 'Nothing, baby,' and, oh God, she goes, 'Mommy, what's the matter, you sad, you mad?' And I'm looking at her, like, you're only 3 years old. She's smart and she's catchy. I wish we had a home. I dream about it. If God gave me the opportunity again, I'd never ever be in this situation again. I'd be a holy saint. If He gave me all the things that I want, and that's nothing but a beautiful home for me and my child and my other child when it gets here, where I'm more settled and I don't have to go to a homeless shelter. . . . I never ever want to be homeless again. I am only 4 months [pregnant]. I'm looking at my stomach—my stomach looks pretty big to me—but I'm still considering an abortion. Because I really am. But then I don't want to. I'm only considering abortion because I'm so mixed up and so homeless. I never wanted a child . . . because I was a workaholic, I worked 9:30 to 6:30 and from 9:00 to midnight. I worked almost to the day I had my daughter, and right now no one will call me."*

Tammy: *"This is the first time in my life I have used a shelter. . . . I think that's what makes it so hard. Because ever since my 9-year-old was born, I have always been able to provide a home for them [her children]. And it really hurts me that I can't give that to them now."*

Sandy: *"I feel really awful that I put my kids in this kind of situation here. . . . Two of my kids spent their birthdays here; they think it's a joke. My son was like, 'You told us 2 weeks when we came here, and now it's been 2 months.' "*

Paula: *"My 3-year-old says, 'Let's go home,' and I say, 'Honey, you don't know, but this is home.' Yeah, I hate to put them in this situation. I thought my mom would let us stay. I had no place else."*

Abiding by the Rules

For most families, the most frequent source of discomfort and frustration associated with shelter living was the shelter rules, such as curfew and the prohibition against corporal punishment of children. Apparently, they perceived these rules as taking away their freedom and dignity and as impeding their efforts to become good parents. In the process of our interviews, we also became aware that the level of frustration varied among the residents of the three shelters (referred to here as shelters A, B, and C). With the exception of the prohibition against corporal punishment of children, these shelters had different rules, covering admission policies, allowed length of stay, curfews, food policies, and so on. The more lenient a shelter's rules were, the lower the sense of frustration and discomfort among its residents.

Shelters A and C did not admit boys age 10 or over or men, and thus only daughters and/or sons under age 10 could accompany their mothers, which sometimes resulted in reluctant and painful separation among family members. On the other hand, shelter B admitted husbands/partners and sons of all ages and encouraged family members to stay together. Curfew was set at 7:30 P.M., 10:30 P.M., and 8:30 P.M. for shelters A, B, and C, respectively. Shelter A mandated all families to attend in-house religious services and encouraged parents to participate in evening Bible study sessions. If a woman showed diligence in participating in the Bible study group, she was promoted to a discipleship and could receive an extension of stay beyond the shelter's prescribed

30-day limit. Shelter A had an in-house school for kindergarten through the eighth grade as well as a primary care clinic, and a uniformed security guard monitored its entrance.

Shelter B did not post a security guard at the door. It provided day care services for 2 1/2 hours in the morning and 2 1/2 hours in the afternoon. Parents were required to leave the shelter premises by 11:00 A.M., supposedly to go out to find housing and take care of other business. They were also required to attend at least two weekly evening group sessions or workshops, on such topics as parenting or drug education. Shelter B also held a weekly meeting between the director and all of the residents. The building in which this shelter was located had been a two-story motel, and its rooms were big enough for two double beds and were all equipped with a private bathroom and shower. In 1996 a major renovation and redecoration of the building was done. When we returned in 1996–1997, we found that the facility provided a much cleaner and more comfortable environment than it had at the time of our earlier interviews in 1994–early 1996. During our 1994–early 1996 interview sessions, we had heard many parents expressing concerns about sanitation at the shelter.

Shelter C was primarily a safe house for domestic violence victims, but it also admitted other homeless mothers with children. Because it was a safe house, residents were not allowed to have visitors. Because of its relatively small size, shelter C had a more homey atmosphere than the other two. Unlike shelters A and B, shelter C sometimes allowed parents to prepare snacks for their children in the kitchen.

All three shelters offered services to help families with finding housing and filling out public assistance applications. They also had limited counseling services. Based on its curfew time, strict adherence to its religious mission, and other rules, shelter A was the most structured and regimented of the three. Overall, shelter B had the most organizational flexibility and offered the widest range of services.

An almost universally expressed frustration had to do with shelter policies that prohibited parents from physically punishing their children. Transition from home to a shelter was tough for both the parents and the children, but especially for the children, the distress of the transition and the adjustment to a shelter was often exhibited in the form of aggravated behavioral problems. Almost unanimously, the parents said that their children had picked up bad behaviors from other children and had become more difficult to control because of the parents' inability to discipline them. It appeared that many parents had used occasional corporal punishment as a disciplinary measure at home and that they valued its utility and effectiveness. Thus, the parents' frustration stemmed not only from the prohibition against spanking per se but also from their inability to maintain consistency and effectiveness in the way they were raising their children. The latter added to their sense of loss of control over their lives:

Erica: "*It's just that your kids need discipline. I mean, I am black, and I don't want my kids in no gangs when they grow up. It starts now. I already lost a brother to the streets. I don't want that for my kids. One day you can't just say, 'Stop.' It starts now.*"

Roseanne: "*My older daughter, since we have been here, she doesn't get too many spankings, because we're not allowed to spank them here, and her mouth is extra spunky. She'll talk back a lot, and she didn't usually do that. They don't let you discipline your kids. They'll give you blue slips, and you get three blue slips, you get kicked out. I can pass up the spanking to have a roof over my head.*"

Margaret: "*Here they say that the staff is my boss and my children listen to the staff, not me, saying they are the boss.*"

Cathy: "*Without a home, you and your child in that home, it hurts. You don't realize how much it has an effect on your child and yourself. You need a home, a place you can call your own, where you can raise your child up. You can't raise your child up being homeless, because you got this person helping you, this person hindering you, and you got other rules you have to abide by. Not to say I don't like other rules, but you have to set boundaries for your child. . . . When you are homeless and you go into someone else's house, it's like you have to go by those rules, and kids see that. Kids are smarter than we realize.*"

Another almost unanimous source of frustration in shelters A and B were policies that did not allow parents to prepare snacks for their children or to bring in food.

Lynn: "*It's just that it's hard here. . . . The rules are so strict. You can't get your WIC [Women, Infants, and Children program vouchers]. I'm trying to feed my kids right with balanced meals, and they tell me if I bring [WIC vouchers] here, I have to give them away to give to other people and I don't appreciate that. I don't appreciate not being able to watch the news at night at least.*"

Erica: "*We can't bring in food. My kids are hungry. Kids shouldn't be hungry. Kids need to eat warm food. We even tried. We wanted to have a snack for the kids each night, and the staff said no, because not everyone has food stamps. But we said we'd chip in and give $10 to those who didn't have. . . . We can't even buy food, so we don't budget. We're supposed to learn to budget, and we can't.*"

Amanda: "*Don't get me wrong. The workers are very pleasant, and I like them all, but I think the rules are too strict. What is it going to hurt to bring in food? No food in the room, I understand, because they have a bug problem. I also understand it causes a problem because not everyone can bring it in, but these kids go to bed starving. . . . My kids [5- and 4-year-olds] are not bad. But they do some things like grabbing for the refrigerator, and that's a cause for a blue slip. I mean, they had had everything taken away in one day. They don't think about it, and they do it. You cannot expect them to forget all their habits."*

The parents in shelter A felt frustrated by the 7:30 P.M. curfew. Marie spoke for the other parents when she told us: *"[Whenever I'm away from the shelter] I'm always on pins and needles. I gotta rush back. I gotta do this. I don't want a point for this. I am constantly thinking on the points that I'll get if I happen to come back past 7:30."*

As to the generally strict rules of shelter A, Karen said: *"I hate living on a schedule that other people have made for me. I like to work on my own time. It's weird. It's kinda like being incarcerated."*

But Holly, a domestic violence victim, said of the curfew and the other rules of shelter B: *"They [the rules] have been fine with me. Just like anywhere you live, you get to follow their rules. You make your rules in your house; they make their rules here. If you can't abide by the rules, then you expect to get disciplined. We appreciate everything they've done for us. We got a roof over our head, we eat three times a day. We come in at 10:00, and to me that's a sufficient amount of time for a female that has children to be in the house anyway."*

Then again, Carol and Brian, a working couple, told us of shelter B rules that required everyone to vacate the premises by mid-morning. Brian said: *"Basically, we hate it here because rules should be in respect to different people's problems. We don't all have the same problems. . . . In the mornings you have to be out by 11:00 until 1:00 or 2:00 P.M. I work nights; occasionally she works nights. Working at night, I'm tired, but I still have to get up and leave. We shouldn't have to leave early in the morning. People who are trying to start over should have different rules. Be more flexible and individualized. Everything else is reasonable. You can definitely save money by staying here. There are some advantages. It's just the time schedule with working late and meals are at certain times. If you work during those hours, you have to eat out and miss out on the meal."*

Others wished for an individualized or flexible approach in other aspects of the shelter programs and services. The uniform application of rules and services apparently added to a sense of humiliation for those who tried to maintain their sense of dignity by disassociating themselves from the rest of the residents.

Louise: *"Rules are fine. It's a shelter, and I don't expect everything to be my way, so it's OK. But everybody that comes to the shelter is not evicted or having a drug problem. We go to these workshops here, and I feel uncomfortable sometimes, because one is to help that you never get evicted again, and I've never been evicted. Another one is on drug counseling or whatever. I never did drugs in my life, and I don't really know nothing about them, so I just sit there. You have to go to a certain number of meetings a week, and I try to pick the ones I think will help me, and I go to one on life skills and it turns out to be drug education. I think they shouldn't treat everyone the same way. They let you down for that, and I feel uncomfortable. I mean, they do an intake and know everybody's situation, so we should not be treated like we're all the same. Even the staff, they assume you're either on drugs or been evicted. And there are people who have been here several times, and I guess you start thinking, but everybody is not the same."*

Noreen, who is a second-time resident of the same shelter and proud of her associate's degree and continuous work history, which had been halted only because of her teenage son's delinquency problems, said:

"About five years ago, it was the [same shelter]. It was domestic violence and, my God, I had never been through something like that. I jumped out a moving car because he said he was going to kill me and he ran over my leg. I'll never forget it. I had to come to the shelter with a cast up over my knee and my baby was only 6 weeks old at the time. Man, when I first came, it was pretty rough. I was banged up. At first, I thought the staff was being kind of cruel, but other women were reaching out. I don't think I stayed too long.

"This time I came to the shelter, they have different things to help the women with. Like, if you're in domestic violence or have drug problems, they have counseling and AA meetings here. I think they're good. I see that they have improved from 5 years ago. But I believe that women might say, like me, I am a college graduate; I do desire to make my life better, and I fell into a situation where I had to come here. I do think that the shelter should try to help women of my caliber who want to do better for themselves or to go to school and help them find resources. To find someone to care about our other needs, not just finding an apartment, can lift self-esteem. So, maybe, if the shelter can help show some resources and bring people in, like, career workshops. . . . "

When Michael said the following, we believed he was speaking for a lot of the homeless parents: *"I want to say something about being homeless. People in this country, I have never seen people get treated the way they do when they are homeless. What I am saying applies to single people too, but when you have a child and they toss you out knowing there is no place for you to go, there is something wrong with that, really something wrong. I know rules and regulations exist for reasons and people can*

*conform and get services, but sometimes rules need to be a little more
lenient or flexible, I should say. One other thing, I don't know, maybe it's
just me, but people who work with the homeless should maybe get a
sensitivity class. They need it."*

Perception of Staff Attitude

In conjunction with their frustration over the loss of control in their
lives, some parents, like Michael, described their perceived humiliation
and indignity at the hands of disrespectful shelter staff and their frustration with the staff members' lack of willingness to help. These parents
felt that some shelter staff had "chips on their shoulders" and very
negative attitudes toward the residents. Others, although frustrated
with the level of assistance, tried hard to put themselves in the staff's
shoes and blamed the contextual factors—too many residents with
multiple needs versus too few staff—as major impediments to a satisfactory level of staff assistance. Still others felt that the staff were caring
and helpful, and they appreciated the staff's assistance.

Because all three shelters operated on a shoestring budget, they
were insufficiently staffed. This meant that staff members were mostly
consumed by managing the daily routines in the shelter and dealing
with the myriad crises among residents. This organizational reality left
little time and energy for the staff to pay close attention to individual
residents. In terms not only of numbers but also of qualifications, the
shelters were not able to employ professionally trained and fully quali-
fied staff who would have been more sensitive toward the mental and
emotional needs of parents and children.

Despite these common problems, the management style in each shelter was distinctive. Thus, the difference in parents' reaction to staff
attitudes tended to reflect each shelter's organizational flexibility, as
found in its rules and requirements; frustration ran high in shelter. A,
where rules tended to be the strictest, and appreciation was more
common in shelters B and C, where the general atmosphere was more
relaxed than in shelter A. Overall, it was our impression that parents
at shelters B and C felt that the staff, including the director, were easily
accessible and felt comfortable expressing their ideas and thoughts to
them, although they might not always have been helpful to a satisfactory
degree, whereas those at shelter B voiced more negative than positive
feelings about the staff and the organization.

Rebecca (shelter A): *"With your self-esteem down, you come into a
shelter and get around the workers that treat you lower than you already*

feel. That's even more hardship on you. It makes you feel that you don't want to get up and do nothing. What are you worth? They treat you like you're garbage, and I mean that makes you feel even worse. I wish the people, whoever is in charge of these shelters, would just come in today and see. Just, I wish they could be a fly on the wall, invisible, and see the certain things that some of us have to go through. . . . You find those people that know how to pull a person down. It's aggravating, it's frustrating. Last week I went to the hospital because I had severe migraines; come to find out it's stress, because I worry about this and I worry about that. And they talk about coming back so you can get reevaluated, just label me clinically depressed. I refuse that."

Esther (shelter B): *"Basically this shelter here is good. But there are so many people here and you might have a serious problem, but the staff just don't have time. Like with me, my public assistance was getting cut and I needed verification for housing. Sometimes you have to wait for somebody, and then it can be too late. They are here to help, but because of the numbers, they can't help like you need it."*

Sandy (shelter B): *"Some of the counselors have been nice. They will listen to you and talk to you. And some of them here, it's just a job and that's it. I am here and I am doing what I have to do and I am leaving and that's all it is. And I hope I'll never be in this situation again in life."*

Angela (shelter B): *"The counselors are really helpful. If you get depressed, you can talk to them. They got a lot of programs that's going on with the help they have, like group sessions that you can go to."*

Many parents' experience of frustration and indignity was not just with shelter staff, but with the helping system in general. We have found, not unexpectedly, that these parents' perception of staff as unwilling and reluctant to help have been compounded by their negative experiences and frustrations with other helping professionals, such as caseworkers, and with staff at other shelters where the parents had previously stayed. They expressed their frustration at their dealings with and their distrust of the welfare, housing, and mental health systems as follows:

Tara: *"At a shelter that I stayed earlier, the housing coordinator gives you just enough information. She knows more, but she'll only give you so much. She is one who pulled out all by herself, and she believed we all should do her way. It's hard to get a lot of information out of people without pulling it out. I guess she wants us to do it on our own. She's the type of person that got to where she's at on her own, and she pushes it off to other people. She did it that way."*

Roseanne: *"My caseworker at DSS didn't want to help me at all. She didn't want to give me benefits. And when she did, she didn't tell me they*

were at the store, so they sat there for like 4 or 5 days. . . . So who knows?
I'm gonna keep bothering them so. At first, I was like, I am not going to
say nothing, but then I saw that if you don't, you get nowhere."

Paula: *"I am trying to get off of PA so hard. I am so sick of the system.*
They are messing around a lot. My caseworker is so nasty."

Michelle: *"[After coming into the shelter] I found out a lot of things I*
didn't know were available. I had to be homeless to find out. My caseworker
didn't volunteer any information to me. Maybe I wouldn't have ended up
homeless if I knew more."

CONCERNS ABOUT THE WELFARE OF CHILDREN

In addition to the issue of discipline that we presented earlier, parents
living in shelters faced barriers to adequately providing for their children's basic needs, such as nutrition, hygiene, clothing, and education.
In shelters A and B, where parents were not allowed to cook or bring
in snacks for their children, they repeatedly talked about their children's
hunger. Especially at shelter B, where dinner consisted of a cold sandwich at 5:00 P.M., parents were frustrated, angry, and sad. They also
reported that the commotion and noise of congregate living disrupted
their children's sleep and that it could have contributed to their restless-
ness and crankiness. Some children we were able to observe during
our interviews indeed looked tired. Sanitation was also a big issue;
keeping children clean and healthy was a struggle. Lack of understanding from teachers and school staff and delays in arranging transportation
to school added to the parents' agony about their children's educational
problems. We were also surprised at the large number of parents who
mentioned lack of clothes for their children as a major problem. Considering their financial status, keeping their growing children properly
clothed was not an easy task, especially in an area where more than half
of the year is winter. Lack of clean clothes and winter gear sometimes
prevented children from attending school.

Most parents also noticed that their children were suffering from
the emotional trauma of being homeless and living in shelters. Young
children became more clingy, and school-age children became either
more hyperactive or more withdrawn. Some teenagers took the situation
in stride, whereas others were having a hard time. For older children,
a sense of shame was definitely a factor. On the other hand, we found
that living in a shelter opened opportunities for some children to participate in activities—summer camp and gym—that they would not have
been able to do in the past and to receive long-overdue health care.

Hunger and Malnutrition

Almost without exception, parents expressed strong feelings about the shelter's providing an inadequate diet for their children. Because of fiscal constraints, these shelters relied heavily on food donated by local grocery chains and restaurants. Apparently, this resulted in a diet that was not always fresh or varied and certainly not like the diet that the children had been accustomed to at home. Some children did not eat, and others, especially the older ones, were constantly hungry because the three poor meals daily did not provide adequate nutrition for their proper physical development.

Sandy: *"Being here, I have lost weight; my son has lost weight—his face looks sunken; all of us [have lost weight]. They feed us old food, and they throw it together. I have seen green bologna, green roast beef. We eat sandwiches day in and day out. Old bread. No nutritious meals. We are hungry more than anything else. I have never been so hungry in my life. I didn't know what it was like to be hungry. My kids were used to eating whenever they wanted to. When I went into the cafeteria the other day, I wanted to cry because they were feeding us the same thing we ate the night before, and I had no money to buy my kids something else. Hard bread and tuna fish for dinner. My baby at night, she cries because her stomach hurts. Some of them even told us they feel bad giving us that food. And another thing is that they get short-staffed and they have a guy clean the building all day and then he serves us the food in the same outfit. He's cleaning sinks and toilet bowls and he's serving our food. My stomach turns.*

"I feel should have a lounge up here. You see, they don't allow us to have any food up here. They should have a place, because a lot of us still get food stamps. OK, let us parents get together and cook for our children. Get three or four of us. They have a big kitchen across the way with a big stove, and they can have one of the counselors watch over us if they don't trust us in the kitchen. But let us cook for our children a nutritious meal."

Tammy: *"They need to do something about the food. My kids were used to eating at least two meals out of the day being hot. They are so sick of sandwiches for supper every night. And because they're sick of it, they're only eating one, and then they're waking up at midnight, one, two in the morning because their tummies hurt. I've got boxes of cereal and they'll eat cereal in the morning until they are full. I don't care how much they eat as long as they're full. And I don't let them waste anything; I'm a penny pincher. But the food here is horrible. The kids are hungry; women have said they're hungry, but they're concerned about their kids. They are going too long without eating. We eat at 5 o'clock, and they aren't fed again until eight in the morning. Come on, it ain't right. And with [her 7-year-old son]* on Ritilin, it curbs his appetite; that's why he's so tiny. I talk to them and all they'll give him is a bowl of cereal. He's used to grabbing something, an apple, a piece of sandwich meat. How much can peanut butter and jelly cost? And the bread they serve here is dry and old. The doughnuts had to be 2, 3 days old. They won't even let us have a fruit basket up here. What's so bad about a fruit basket? It's healthy. I don't care about me, but the kids shouldn't have to eat that way."

Amanda: "My kids won't eat this food. I mean, they'll go a day without eating and just drink juice. The food is nasty. It is disgusting. Kids don't know what they're doing, but they're starving themselves in a way, and that's a cause for them to go and call CPS [Child Protective Services] on a mother. My kids, I don't give them candy or sweets or even butter. They'll eat the cereal, but they're sick of bologna for the first 5 days."

Brenda: "They are just used to going in the refrigerator when they wanted. Fixing their own cereal when they get up; they miss that. They say they are hungry but can't eat now. Now they have to get up to eat or they will be hungry."

Health and Sanitary Problems

As shown in chapter 2, homeless children had many severe chronic health problems, most of which—high lead levels and resulting developmental disabilities, attention deficit disorders, speech problems, ear problems, stomach disorders, asthma, and skin problems—could be traced to poverty and poor living environments in inner-city neighborhoods. A chaotic transition from home to shelter, stress associated with the move, school change, disruption in daily routines, and hunger at the shelter all no doubt aggravate the children's health problems. Also, parents told us that, because of the congregate and crowded living conditions at the shelter, children were more prone to develop various acute ailments (ringworms, colds, and other infectious diseases).

Sandy: "I feel really awful that I put my kids in this kind of situation here. You know, you're living in a place where you don't know who you're around. You don't know these people. People have different germs. It's kind of creepy here. I have to use my sheets; my kids won't get under the ones here. I have seen too many people get sick here. I keep my room as clean as I can, but the place is filthy. There are fleas jumping around on the rug in the lounge. There are kids here, and it hurts me. We can't wash our clothes; I've been asking for 4 days. They have only one washing machine in a facility across the street, and we have to wait for someone [to open the facility]. Children need clean clothes. And that upsets me *really, really bad. Because we're homeless, everybody is not dirty or trashy. I teach my kids: We don't have a lot, but what you have, keep it clean. The fact that we are homeless doesn't make us bums. Not everybody's a bum. There are some people that came in, and I watch them and you can tell I'm not like that."*

Fortunately, following its renovation and redecoration, shelter B became a cleaner, more pleasant environment. The parents we interviewed in late 1996 and early 1997 in fact indicated that the place was "sanitary," and no one expressed dissatisfaction regarding the physical environment, except that the rooms had only a shower, not a bathtub, making it hard to bathe younger children. Nevertheless, the crowding did not abate, and parents expressed concerns about *"children coughing on one another"* and their not being able to get enough sleep because of the shelter noise. The parents' biggest concerns for their children's health, however, came from the worsening of existing problems, the aggravation apparently caused by the stress and trauma of being homeless.

Jennifer: *"Even though he's young [9 months old], I don't think he's very comfortable here. He's not used to having 5 million people around. He'd sleep better at home. If someone slams a door or something, he wakes up."*

Jacqueline: *"You know, you got new people coming in, old people leaving, and kids running around, roughhousing and stuff, a lot of noise and a lot of commotion for him [7 1/2 months old] [to have proper rest]."*

David: *"My 4-year-old has asthma, and it had gotten worse since we came here. The other one, he's not eating like he used to. He'd beg for food; he used to eat half a loaf of bread. His health has deteriorated a bit. I am really worried about them."*

Trauma of and Adjustment to Homelessness

In addition to exacerbated physical health problems, homeless children exhibited multiple psychosocial problems due apparently to the stress and trauma of homelessness. A significant proportion of children had preexisting psychosocial and behavioral problems such as attention deficit disorders or hyperactivity, bed wetting, and sleep disorders. After the children came to the shelter, many of their existing problems became aggravated. Parents also frequently identified acting out and fighting, withdrawal or the tendency to get upset or cry easily, and the tendency to cling to them as problems that emerged or intensified at the shelter. Loss of familiar surroundings and routines, with the resulting sense of insecurity, created difficulty in adjusting to a shelter for almost all children, and their stress showed up as behavioral problems. It appeared that, for many children, the loss of their home was only one of many losses that they had already experienced, including separation from their fathers, siblings, and/or other relatives, the death of a family member, especially a grandmother, with whom they had had a close relationship, and frequent moving. Moving into a shelter also often separated family members, and mothers frequently mentioned that their children missed their fathers, siblings, and grandparents who did not accompany them to the shelter. Several mothers also volunteered the information that their children had been physically abused by their father/stepfather and that the experience had left a scar. There were also children who had allegedly been sexually abused by adults.

Younger children did not understand why they were not allowed to do certain things they had been used to, and thus they were confused and frustrated. Some children were also aware that infractions of the rules would lead to the family's expulsion from the shelter, and they felt inhibited by and terrified of those rules. This certainly added to their sense of anxiety and insecurity. Older children frequently expressed their frustration and anger about the situation by defying their parents and by getting into fights at school. Parents also reported that their older children were embarrassed about the family's homelessness and were having a tough time dealing with their sense of shame. Many just tried to "*stuff their feelings in.*" It was no wonder that many children with multiple traumas and a pervasive sense of loss, anxiety, frustration, anger, and shame had serious psychosocial problems. Judging from the parents' report, we believe that many children were depressed and needed counseling.

Although children needed increased parental attention at the shelter, the reality was that their parents, being in crisis, were also stressed out, having to deal with their own emotional turmoil and the search for housing. The emotionally and physically worn-out parents often were not able to meet their children's emotional needs adequately.

Patti: "*There's a lot more whining. The 9-year-old whines all the time, and she complains all the time. They need more of my attention, but I've been focusing on what we really need as far as getting by and having a place to live.*"

Angela: "*My son, he's anemic and he has, like, relapsed. He was potty trained, and he went from being potty trained backwards to wetting himself again.*"

Barbara: "*He [1-year-old] gets upset and cries just being around people, lots of people. It's been hard here sometimes, because it's kind of overwhelming.*"

Lynn: *"She [3-year-old] is out of character since she's been here. It's like she knows that she's been displaced or something."*

Marie: *"[Her 4-year-old daughter] is a real peaceful girl. I would say, in the way of wanting her own place, she's, she's like mourning for that. She wants her own room back. She misses her father, because her father spends a lot of time with her. And by her slowly not seeing her daddy around, they are slowly starting to think, because children aren't stupid, 'Why are we in the position we are in?' They don't know everything, but they are starting to see. . . . "*

Wilma: *"I have noticed that she [9-year-old] is regressing some. It's like 'Mommy, Mommy' all the time. I think her house is gone, and now she wants to make sure her parents don't disappear. She needs stability, that we will have a home and we will stick together and that we're still a family."*

Tammy: *"It's the older one [9-year-old] I worry about the most, because she stuffs her feelings away. The other day, she said, 'Mommy, I am scared.' She knows that if they do something wrong, it can get written up here, and after a certain number of times we wouldn't have a place. She knows. She's very intelligent. She's not bonding with any other kids here. She's getting up there where she understands all that. And she feeds off me if I am feeling something."*

Sandy: *"I know they're getting really homesick for New York and their grandparents and everything. . . . I felt real bad to see my daughter cry last night. She was crying so hard. It's like she had been holding it in. And when I asked her if she's all right, she just said she was missing her daddy and Aunt Valerie. I try and take them out, away from here, but you see I don't know lots of people. For my oldest son, I sit and I talk to him to try and get him to open up more. I mean, he gets along with people; he doesn't fight with anybody. But I want to know what's on his mind more because he's very, very quiet. I don't know—maybe I'm not doing it right. They are definitely going through something, and I am too. . . . I lived in East Harlem most of my life, and it's not real bad, but it's ghettolike. When I moved upstate, my main thing was that we are going to live good. I didn't know much about [this city]. I still don't know much. And when I did get around, they just took me to the worst areas, and [this city] was nothing but a big ghetto."*

Marian: *"My [15-year-old] son doesn't like it here, because they have rules and regulations that are different from at home. He can't have his own key, or just lay in bed or raid the refrigerator. . . . He was in the [homeless youth shelter] for like a week and a half when I was staying with my friend. When I got lucky and got a room here, he didn't want to come. But I'm trying to keep us together. . . . I had to go to school for him. He had a confrontation with a substitute teacher. He's starting to get in trouble and talk back. He's been going to [magnet school for honors students] since the fifth grade and now he's in the tenth, and this is taking a toll on him. He's going through a lot."*

Esther: *"The 6-year-old, at first he was getting into fights and now he won't come out of his room. He even refuses to come out and eat. There was a lady here with her son and he was so bad. He was cussing at my son, and my son told her [the boy's mother] and she did nothing. They went into the TV room, and the next thing I realized was she was yelling and screaming and pointing at my son with her finger in his face. I went in and said, 'If you have a problem with him, you can come to me,' trying to talk to her. She was on medication, and there was something wrong with her and she almost got into [physical outbursts]. So maybe he figures he'll stay up there."*

Donna: *"None of them wanted to be here when we first got here. After a few days went by, they adjusted, but they are more sad than usual. My 13-year-old had to spend her birthday here. She cried and cried. My son, my baby, is extra-hyper."*

Carol and Brian: *"They hate it here; no porch. Or they just want to go outside and play and there's no place here to do that. They become irritable, and then they fight with each other."*

Chris: *"My 10-year-old, my daughter, she doesn't like it here. She's getting very mouthy with me; same thing with my son. They are hard to control, and they know they can get away with it. It's like, you can't send them to their room, because you'd have to go too, and you're punishing yourself. It's tough unless they're sleeping. . . . [At home] my 2-year-old can run around, have her toys, have her little freedom. Usually I have snacks for her, and she can run around and nibble once in a while. Here she can't. I try to explain it to her, and she doesn't understand. She says, 'I want to go home.' I say, 'soon.' "*

Erica: *"I holler at them a lot. The older one [a 4 1/2-year-old] knows I'm stressed. But my daughter whines more and cries a lot. Before this [homelessness] she was fine, and now she's glued to me. Kids, they get it all."*

Amanda also told us that her children were called names and taunted for their mixed ethnicity and that her 5-year-old started to realize the negative tone: *"Mind you, their father is white. And they get called zebras, and one boy calls them niggers. She's really sensitive with the name calling and stuff, but there's nothing I can do about it. There's nothing you can do to defend your children here."*

Some children are quite resilient and have been able to adjust to the shelter environment as time has gone by. But we have also observed that they needed their parents' hope and reassurance that the situation would get better and that they would be in their own home soon. The fact that Beverly was working and saving for their own home and actually had scheduled a date for them to move into their own apartment apparently helped assuage her 10-year-old daughter's adjustment difficulty: "*When we first came here, she wasn't adjusting too good. I guess she missed her home and the food she likes to eat and what we used to do. We would go to the library, or she would ride her bike, play video games, watch TV, or play outside. . . . Now she's open. She feels like she's at home. Like when we went shopping she said, 'When are we going home?' She's playing with the other kids now. Before, it was just with me.*"

Brenda also told us that her children were having less difficulty in adjusting to the shelter because "*I tell them it is temporary and they are encouraged because I go looking for housing and tell them this person called and this person called. They feel, you know, they are just looking forward to getting their own. . . . They feel comfortable here. We go walking and they say, 'When are we going home?*' "

The psychosocial problems of children who have seen domestic violence ran deeper. Mothers noticed a lot of anger in their children. Mothers also had serious concerns about them because "*they have seen a lot of things they should not have.*"

Elaine: "*[Her boys] have seen things they never should have seen. They, we, need counseling. They shouldn't have seen a man trying to rape their mom, shooting at their mom. . . . I don't think it will just go away. I don't want them to have nightmares.*"

Hilary: "*It's hard for them to understand and to deal with it. Kids don't want to feel hurt, and now they're separated from their sister and it bothers them. Kids forget for a while, and then it flashes back. [Her little boy] has seen it and it hurts him. He wants to know why it's that way.*"

Nevertheless, the mothers also reported that their children felt safe at the shelter.

Jan: "*They love being here. They'd rather be here than where we were. They know that, when we're here, Mom's cooler and relaxed. I am not a wreck like I was when we got here. They saw a man hurting their mother. They have seen so much violence. They ask me if he's going to live with us again and all that. But we are happier without him.*"

Frances: "*Initially it seemed like they lacked attention. . . . Their teacher and I are pretty close, and she said they were kinda gone. Who knows what's on their minds. Now it's a big relief for them. It seems like they took a big breath and it's fine. The surroundings, you know, are a lot better . . . the pressure is not there. Before, they were left with him and they couldn't relax and do what kids should be able to do. They had seen these things happen and now they know I'm safe. What they saw wasn't right. They ask me questions. Last time my older son asked me, 'How many times did he hit you?' I have had a busted lip and black eye, and I would say things to patch it up. . . . It had happened too many times. I have enlisted in counseling to ease their minds."*

Insensitivity of School Staff and Other Educational Problems

School-age homeless children were experiencing even more hardship because of the insensitivity of both the school system and the people who work in the system. Administrators and teachers whose job is to educate deprived children in inner-city schools have many barriers to doing their job well. These inner-city schools suffer from inadequate funding, aging buildings, crowded classrooms, and so forth, and the administrators and teachers who try to do their best to educate poor children deserve praise for their dedication and commitment. Unfortunately, however, some teachers and school staff were insensitive to the homeless children's psychoemotional needs and contributed to, rather than alleviating, the trauma and sense of shame that the children experienced. Parents trying to send their children to the same school in their old neighborhood also expressed frustration at the school system's unresponsiveness to or tardiness in responding to the need for transportation arrangements for the children.

For homeless children, who experience so much disruption in their residential and family life, school may be the only place where they can find some consistency and seek a refuge, albeit temporary, from the chaos of homelessness. As overburdened as they already are, the school administrators and teachers are still the logical people to provide support and to help the children with their academic and emotional needs. At minimum, the educators must realize that these children, who face multiple barriers to success, need as many sensitive and caring adults as possible if they are to do more than just get through a day. Some children will be resilient and will grow up, with parental support alone, without much of a problem despite the multiple barriers, but others need much support and guidance from parents, teachers, and other adults.

Yolanda: *"The kids at school rag him [her 11-year-old son] all the time because the teachers say things so the kids know he's in a shelter. . . . He went to get a bus pass, and the [school] secretary said real loud, 'He lives in a shelter,' with all the other people around. I went in and talked to a counselor. I told her I am worried about my son's morale. He's there to learn. I told them my son is in a place that the secretary ain't never seen. He shouldn't have to deal with that. You're trying to build him up, and some people step in and can ruin it for you. . . . We talk and I tell them [her children] about the importance of education. I show them the bums on the street and say it will be them without an education. It's harsh, but it's true. They need an education; they need a job. I tell them all the time. We stick together, we do a lot of praying, and I'm beating the streets every day. They need a home. A home! I think they'd be ecstatic if they had their own home."*

Louise (who moved from another city): *"My kids used to love school, but my son does not like it so much here because he says the teacher hits the kids with a stick and the teacher's aide uses her hand. He was traumatized. He was like, 'Mommy, did you get hit when you went to school?' He just can't cope with it. I'm going to the teacher Monday because I thought corporal punishment had been done away with in schools. There's another little boy and girl here in his class, and they all say it and they know where the teacher hides, or puts, the stick. I mean if I hit him with a stick and the teacher asks him if I hit him, then she's gonna call CPS, and I feel like I should talk to her and then maybe call it on her."*

Bonnie: *"His [7-year-old son's] teacher isn't very good. It's just, anybody who can yell at kids 8 hours a day isn't a good teacher. She doesn't talk to any of them. She just keeps saying he's being bad, but when you are yelling at a kid all day . . . "*

Terri: *"We have been having trouble with [her 13-year-old son's] school. Unfortunately, they put the address at my mom's instead of using this one [the shelter]. He's been walking, but I think by Monday it will be cleared up. But he wants me to keep walking him to the corner instead of being picked up in front of the shelter; he's ashamed of this. He doesn't want others to know he's here. He's having a hard time with this."*

Sue: *"We had to fill in a transportation transfer, and they say it usually takes a couple of weeks. But there was another family here and their children went to the same school. So I popped over to the school to leave her bus fare one morning, and I stopped to see the assistant principal. We had an argument, but eventually he let her ride the bus the same day."*

Wilma: *"I had a little problem with that [arranging for her daughter to stay in the same school] when we first got here. The bus driver tried to make her feel bad about being in the shelter. . . . They didn't bring her home and then forgot to pick her up."*

Mary: *"It took, maybe, like 2 weeks [for the bus to come]. He [her son] went every day, though; I took him on the bus. But his grades are slipping, and I would imagine what it's from."*

Out of 80 families we interviewed, only a few owned a car. Chris's family was one of them, but Chris still experienced difficulty with her children's transportation: "*[Before coming to the shelter] we were at a motel in the Sheridan Drive area and I was driving them, but then the car broke down and I told them [the school officials] and they didn't arrange nothing. So they [her children] didn't go to school for a couple of weeks.*"

In the case of Danielle, who had been moving back and forth among friends' and relatives' houses, the barrier to sending her 5-year-old son to school was not only the lack of transportation but also the lack of a permanent address: "*When he went to [a suburban school] he had a transportation problem, so he was out for a couple of months for that. But they really kicked him out because he didn't have a permanent residence, which I thought was pretty wrong. The principal told me that he could no longer go there because he had no permanent residence.*" Although the Stewart B. McKinney Act made illegal the denial of school attendance to a child for lack of a permanent residence, some school administrators apparently were not paying attention to the law or to the educational needs of homeless children. It appeared that the principal in question was not willing to arrange transportation every time Danielle and her boy changed their residence. He may have thought it was too much of an inconvenience and just wanted to get out of it.

Lack of proper school clothes was not a minor problem either. Patti, who, with her six children, came to a shelter without as much as a suitcase to flee her abusive husband, told us in earnest that her children "*missed school quite a few days because they had nothing clean to wear.*" As the weather turned cold, the lack of winter gear for her children was a real problem for Heather: "*[The shelter director] said they have to go to school, but they can't go in the weather because they don't have the gear, you know, hats and gloves and stuff. I said I'll send them, but she's responsible if they get sick and she said, 'No.' . . . They'll go when they get [clothes].*"

Advantages of Shelter Life

Although an absolute majority of the children were having a tough time adjusting to shelter living, we also heard from some parents who said that their children had more opportunities to participate in activities and programs than they had back in their old neighborhood. Child care services at shelter B, in-house health care clinic services at shelter A, and after-school programs such as gym and summer camp programs provided by both shelter A and shelter B were the examples given.

Betty, who had worked an 8-hour day at Burger King before she and her 9-year-old daughter left their rented apartment, said: "*Matter of fact, I think she [her daughter] likes it here because she gets to go to camp and a lot of other things that she couldn't get into while we were living over there at our previous address. She's a lot more active. She got a lot more things to keep her occupied. The reason why she couldn't get into them was because I didn't know anything about them. When you come into the shelter, everything opens up for you. Everything is available for you. You get to know all of these different programs they have.*"

The programs and services for children were part of the resources that many parents had no knowledge of before they came to a homeless shelter. Other parents had known that the services were available, but they had not been able to utilize them due to other barriers or life circumstances. For example, the staff at shelter C found that Maria had delivered her 1-year-old at home and had never taken him to a doctor even for vaccinations. Maria explained that at the time of her divorce 3 years earlier she had given custody of her seven children to their father "*because of financial and educational reasons. [Her ex-husband] has money; he can give them the best of everything. Why should they be on welfare when they've got a father with a lot of money? He's a [professional occupation]. He's spending money going traveling with his girlfriend, and why can't he spend some caring for his children? But the social worker couldn't understand why I wanted to give the children to their father. And she said, 'Well, if you don't want your children, then you don't want the baby you are carrying.' So I had to hide the pregnancy. I didn't tell her when I was delivering or nothing like that. I was scared that they would take [the baby] away. In New York City they have a policy that when you go in [a clinic], they have to see birth certificates and everything in order to give them shots. I don't have any.*" Maria was quite relieved when she was told that the baby would be issued a birth certificate and be taken to a doctor without her having to give him up.

We were also told by some parents that their children were more involved in schoolwork because the shelter environment was actually better than their old neighborhood environment, where the roughness and temptations of its streets negatively affected them. This was especially true in shelter C, a safe house with a homey atmosphere. Judy said the following about her 12-year-old: "*It seemed that living in an emergency shelter brought her grades up. I guess it's because where we were at she was always wanting to go outside and play with the other kids out there. And they chased her around, and she wanted to be like the other girls and she was ready to fight anybody. She wasn't into school. Since we came to the shelter, her grades started to going up from C's to B's and A's.*

She's doing well. I guess it's also because she receives more attention from the other adults who are here. They take up time with her, sit and play games and stuff like that, and she likes it."

Sadly enough, rough and restrictive as it was, the shelter environment was indeed an improvement over what some children had been subjected to, as we have discussed in the case of the children of domestic violence victims. Children who had to experience other types of abusive situations also felt relieved and more comfortable in the shelter than in their previous living situation. Brenda told us that her six children, although they were being crammed together sharing a single room in the shelter, still felt better off because "*they are not in an environment where they're getting cursed at, scared to use the bathroom without getting yelled at.*" She was referring to the doubled-up living situation where her children had been verbally and emotionally abused by her friend and host. Brenda's children had also experienced a couple of other episodes of residential instability before they doubled up with the friend.

Lack of Counseling Services for Children at the Shelter

Despite the multiple psychosocial problems that the homeless children experience at the shelter and the schools, we found that their mental health needs were not being addressed. Mothers who were domestic violence victims unanimously expressed their desire for counseling for their children. Their concern for the children's psychoemotional health was such that they tended to list counseling, rather than a home, as their children's top-priority need. Many other homeless parents who were not domestic violence victims also frequently expressed their desire for counseling for their children who exhibited signs of mental health problems. Unfortunately, the shelters neither provided counseling services for children nor actively referred or linked them to outside services. Only a few children were reportedly receiving counseling at school for their behavior problems.

The reality is that short-staffed temporary shelters are already overextended and are not able to meet the mental health needs of homeless children (or adults in many cases). Among other reasons, their staff usually lack expertise in child psychology. However, homeless children are going through an ordeal that they are most likely incapable of handling by themselves, and staff members must be made aware of this. Mental health services need to be provided in some way. Especially for the older children, who appeared to have an even tougher time than the younger ones, their sense of shame, frustration, and anger is likely to have lasting negative effects on their psychoemotional well-being.

RELATIONSHIP AMONG RESIDENTS

Before we began our interviews, we did not have much of a preconcep-
tion about what the interaction or relationship among homeless families
in the shelter would be like. First of all, we thought, since many families
were coming in and leaving, with some staying for a very short time,
the families might not have the to get to know one another well. Second,
we reasoned, these families were in a crisis so that they might not have
the time and energy to establish a relationship or camaraderie even if
they shared common space. There might be tension among families
because of their high stress level and the crowded space. Moreover,
under the brutal weight of the rough-and-tough realities of life, some
parents might find it hard to trust strangers. On the other hand, we
thought that these families might draw together and share a sense of
solidarity because they were in a similar situation. In the process of
interviewing, we realized that most families chose to stay away from
the other families and that there indeed was more tension than solidarity
among them. It appeared that, because the families felt very much
stigmatized by their homelessness, they even avoided mingling with
other homeless families so as not to affirm their homeless status. To
maintain their sense of dignity, the families stood alone and tried to
differentiate themselves from other "undesirable" or "unworthy" residents. One barometer that we found some parents employing to distance
themselves from the others was the degree of manifestation of self-
help. Many parents expressed downright resentment toward those they
perceived to be not trying hard enough to help themselves. The parents'
perception of lack of self-help among the other parents was often based
on the latter's continued substance abuse and other behavioral indica-
tors of "laziness":

Angela: *"If you do what you are supposed to do, the counselors will go
to the limit for you. If you don't do your job, why go looking for them for
help when you don't want to help yourself? You can't just sit around and
don't want to help yourself and expect people to come to you and say,
'Oh, I got this for you. I got this for you.' No, you got to get up and do it
on your own. They can't get you an apartment. You got to go out there and
find one."*

Holly: *"I am learning a lot. You meet different people; you see different
things. And some things can be worse than your situation, and it makes
you appreciate yourself and your family more. . . . If you come here to help
yourself, that's what you should do. But if you come here just to continuously
do the same things you're in here for. . . . In other words, if you were a
homeless person and you lost your home because of drugs or just something*

*unnecessary that shouldn't have happened and you come here and [are]
not trying to improve yourself, it's a waste of time. Because you are gonna
wind up back here or at another shelter. Why bother? You might as well
stay out here in the same situation you were in. . . . You have freedom
here. You can go out; you can come in. But why try to take away your
freedom because of your own stupidity? And then get mad and say, 'I don't
want to do this. They want you to do this; they want you to do that.' Well,
why did you come here? You knew what you were coming into before you
got here."*

Of course, the parents shared common concerns regarding certain
shelter policies (e.g., prohibition of bringing in food for their children)
and tried to present alternatives as a group to the shelter administration.
In most other aspects of shelter living, however, we did not find a visible
sign of mutual help among families. For most families, since this was
one of the most trying times of their lives, it appeared that they would
attempt to leave it behind as soon as they could and would not wish
to look back. It appeared as if they did not want to carry a trace of the
shelter with them, and thus they made an almost conscious effort not
to establish a bond with anyone who would remind them of the pains
of homelessness.

EVALUATION OF SHELTER LIVING: BENEFITS AND COSTS

In order to find out what the parents thought about the overall effects
their stay at the shelter were having on their lives, we asked them to
provide personal comments on gains or losses that they had experienced since their entry into the shelter. A majority of parents said that
the benefits of the shelter outweighed the problems they had encountered there and that they valued such benefits. Their comments were
largely centered on tangible benefits from services provided by the
shelter: information, referral, and advocacy from staff to aid their home-
finding efforts and application for welfare benefits, and in-house programs such as day care, workshops, GED classes, and linkages to employment training programs. But they also expressed a sense of
empowerment that they had come to possess because of the variety of
information and resources made available at the shelter. At minimum,
they felt that they had picked up some valuable tips that would make
them more skillful in navigating in the rough and tumble outside world.

Because the shelter staff are more likely to be immersed in dealing
with a myriad of day-to-day crisis situations faced by the homeless
families, their one-on-one counseling services were limited in scope,

mostly consisting of short-term, task-oriented sessions. Considering the multiple problems that homeless families have, these counseling services may not be enough even to make a ripple on the surface of most families' lives. Nevertheless, some parents also mentioned the beneficial outcomes of such in-house counseling services. We found that even a little bit of personal attention, respect, and trust showed by the shelter staff to these parents was something that moved and encouraged them; this was not a surprise, given that most of these parents had been shouldering the burden of their poverty and related problems without much support from anyone.

Wilma: *"It's been very positive here. When you come in, you're so distraught. They [the staff] give you help here. They help tell you what to say to landlords, what to check for. . . . We get top priority in housing by being in the shelter. I had pictures of what I thought a shelter would be like, but it has been real helpful."*

Sue: *"For homeless families, a shelter is a place to come to. You can find resources and counselors. If you have a counselor or someone official working with you, it's with that other voice you get more accomplished. You can walk in alone and get nothing, but if you have a counselor call, your chances are better. There is so much out there, but if you don't have another person speaking for you, you will never find out about them, you know, and I think that's kind of sad. If they have all these resources and I call as a homeless person, I can't get help, but if a counselor calls, it gets set up right away. I really appreciate all they've done for me. I found an apartment and generally pulled myself together, and there is a difference. I stayed at another shelter. I won't mention the name of it, but the staff there is not as involved in the people's needs. When I left the other shelter, if I had someone take an interest in me, maybe I would have succeeded then. Here they let you find possibilities."*

Linda: *"There's a lot of people that come and go. Some are—sometimes you get some strange people, you know. I feel uncomfortable. Other than that, it is a good place, clean environment, a place for people who want to do something for themselves. It's great because they will watch your kids while you try to find a place and get your things together. They try to help you get the things you don't have."*

Jessica: *"When I first came here, I was feeling uncomfortable. There was a lot of people, and sometimes I like to have my own space with my child. It's OK here; it's sanitary. You have your own room and bathroom. The only problem is the food. Sometimes the milk is spoiled. Some of the staff have attitudes, and they come in and take it out on you. But I like it. I appreciate it now. I am in parenting classes and GED classes, and I'm going to the workshops they have—art. They have extra food, diapers if you need it.*"

Holly: "*This is a place where you can think. To me, it's just like a penitentiary. I don't mean in a way as being confined or anything. Being here is like you got your own room to get your mind together and be able to think. But then again, like I said, some people don't think. They are just there for the meals and the shelter.*"

Sherry: "*When I was at my apartment, I was going through a lot. . . . Since I came here, it's been an improvement. I learned a lot. Staff here like [name of the director] really care about you and your family. I didn't think it would be like this. She gave me and my kids a second chance, and I appreciate a lot.*"

Heather: "*I am trying to get into this medical secretary program, plus get my GED. I am not trying to sit on welfare my whole life. I've been on it for a long time, and it's time to get off. It makes you lazy and makes you not want to do working. Welfare is a good program, but just to build you so far, and letting you stay on and on is a crippler for everyone. . . . I think this place has been good because we had good talks. My sister came here, and I couldn't understand why would you ever come to a homeless shelter. But she went for herself and now she's doing better and I understand it.*"

But a small minority of parents did not want to take advantage of shelter services or consider that they had any beneficial effect on them. For example, Marie said: "*I try not to lean on them [staff and shelter services] very much, because I know I'm in the system for a short time and because I want to get out of it.*" Her fierce sense of independence was apparently rooted in her pride as someone who had just fallen briefly from her lower-middle-class status. Her husband had already recovered his old job, and she had every reason to feel confident that the family would do well on its own.

The negative evaluation by Cindy, a 22-year-old mother of two, may also have been rooted in her pride. Compared to the majority of parents, Cindy, a full-time college sophomore who also had a stable part-time job, was less likely to value the programs and services that are geared to those with a lower level of education and independence. As a domestic violence victim who came to the shelter, leaving her 3-year-old daughter behind with the child's father, she needed counseling services more than referrals to employment training or group sessions geared to those addicted to illegal drugs. Thus, the mismatch between her needs and the shelter programs may have been a cause of her anger and resentment toward shelter staff, whom she perceived as insensitive and haughty: "*The clients help each other more than the staff. They have attitudes, and we're already stressed. They are not understanding or consid-erate. They have chips on their shoulders. Just a couple of people you can talk to, but they have no authority. When you have to go downtown [DSS], they don't give you bus tokens. If you don't get funding, you have to leave. And the food for kids isn't right. If the kids don't eat, they don't have a substitute. They don't give me any help."*

In the case of Amanda, another 22-year-old mother of three, it ap-peared that her negativism was largely influenced by her interaction with some families whose racial discrimination against her and her children, who were half white and half black, hurt and infuriated her. Given that Amanda had ended up in a shelter because of racism in an all-white neighborhood where she had chosen to live because of her dedication to her children's education, racism in the shelter must have aggravated her stress and anger. She told us that she had once talked to a staff member about the name calling and that the staff member had done nothing about it. So, between racism and a lack of response from the staff, Amanda felt that the shelter was not a place to which she should have turned for help even under the circumstances: *"I don't see how people can get comfortable here and stay for 6 weeks or 3 months. There's nothing like your own. At home, I don't have to listen to no one's mouth, and at home, my kids can play with their toys. At home, they had room, and here they stay up in the room between being called niggers. You got crack heads around; I've been robbed twice, and another lady saying she's gonna cut me in front of my kids. I want them to be safe, and I hate this place. I can't stay here. It sucks in here, and I'm not staying here too much longer."*

6

After the Shelter: Where to Go?

At the time of our interviews, some parents had found housing for their families and were ready to leave the shelter, but most were still trying to find decent housing. In this chapter, we report on the different state of minds of the finders and the seekers and their subjective perception and experience of barriers to finding decent housing and stability.

When we asked the question Where do you think you will be living 6 months from now? we heard a quick reply of "in my apartment" or "in my own house" from the finders. The sense of stability was sinking in, and most appeared to relish it, at least for the time being. We found a sense of relief and hope, although the units that they found might not have been what they really wanted. However, from the seekers, who were languishing for months at the shelter without a clue as to when their good luck would strike, we found a deep sense of confusion, frustration, despair, and hopelessness. They sounded exhausted, and they needed help with their search for housing. Indeed, one common theme that we found among the seekers was their sense of resignation and their tendency to accept their lot in life, their substandard status; another theme was a cry for help.

Both the finders, with the exception of a few who had found what they wanted, and the seekers expressed frustration with what they perceived as barriers to finding decent housing and with their choices, which were limited by those barriers. The overriding themes in their quest for housing were a safe environment for their children and afford-ability. The parents were well aware of the reality that, given their past experience in the local housing market, the prospects for finding a combination of these two would be almost nil. Under the circumstances, public housing and Section 8 units were almost without exception at the top of their wish list, because, if nothing else, they would be af-fordable and would have better building maintenance than most unsub-sidized units. (Paula: "*I want all the lights and gas, because without them, it takes a lot of money, and I don't have it. That's why I want [a public housing project].*" Roseanne: "*Limited funds; that's the only reason I want to move into the projects, because I can't afford to move somewhere else and pay rent with nothing else included. I can't afford it, so it's my only choice.*") Nevertheless, the long waiting list and fierce competition for these subsidized rental units made them out of the reach of most home-less families. Although domestic violence victims and those who had been evicted were given priority for these units, priority status did not guarantee that they would be given the housing, because there was still a waiting list among the priority group. Also, once a family was given a public housing unit, they could not afford to be choosy, because the local public housing authority's policy dictated that, if the family did not accept what they were assigned, they would be moved to the bottom of the waiting list. Because most public housing projects are located in impoverished areas where drugs and violence are commonplace, some families actually turn down the offer of a unit. One parent told us that when she went to inspect a ground-floor public housing unit to which she had just been assigned, she witnessed "*nothing but drug dealers down there.*" She turned down the offer, and according to the take-it-or-lose-it policy of the public housing authority, her application was withdrawn by the public housing authority and she had to submit an-other. In the end, only a small proportion of shelter residents were accepted into the subsidized units. Many families were forced to give up their hope for a subsidized unit and move on to find an unsubsidized unit, relying on their own resourcefulness, checking newspaper ads for private rental units, and walking around. Those who left their substan-dard housing to come to a shelter in the hope of getting a higher spot on the waiting list for public housing or a Section 8 unit were frequently disappointed when they learned that homelessness in itself no longer conferred priority status for one of these units.

In addition to these first-tier structural barriers—the shortage of sub-sidized low-income housing and the deteriorating quality of housing and life in urban areas—the homeless families told us about other barriers that restricted their choices. Most of these other barriers, such as inadequate income, lack of transportation, and unscrupulous landlords preying upon poor people, are also structural in nature, and their alleviation calls for public policy intervention.

FINDERS AND SEEKERS

The most contented finders were no doubt those who were accepted into the public housing. Although some projects were known for rampant drug dealing, others included the newly renovated units that most low-income families covet. Louise considered herself lucky: "*I'm just waiting for a police check to come back so they can see if I've ever been arrested. So, it should be like 15 days. It [the apartment] is right across the street from my mother. I got really lucky; it's public housing. I haven't seen it yet, but it has a kitchen, living room, and three bedrooms, so I'm glad. I'd say I had good luck because the houses here are really bad. They are rundown and they got rats, and landlords here are not good landlords. So, with public housing you get maintenance and all that, and I wanted to live out near my mom.*"

Those who had not been so lucky as Louise but had found a private rental unit also looked forward to their moving into it, although their excitement was somewhat guarded. Mary said: "*Well, the apartment I found is decent inside and everything. I looked at a couple and they were yuk, but I didn't have to take any of those. Truthfully, I'm not totally satisfied. But it is a two-bedroom apartment, and it has a living room, kitchen, bathroom, and basement. So, as of now, I should be satisfied.*"

Most seekers were also resigned to their lack of choice. As Jennifer put it: "*I will probably end up in the [same inner-city neighborhood in which she lived before]. That's not where I want to be, but that's probably where I'll end up.*" A few showed confusion or total despair as to their future whereabouts. Barbara said: "*I am very confused about [where I am going to be in 6 months]. I was thinking about moving back to New York City; I can't even say. I might not even be alive 6 months from now.*"

Those who were staying at the shelter for as long as 2 or 3 months were even more frustrated and cried for help.

Cathy: "*Honey, I hope to be settled in [public] housing or an apartment with my new baby and my daughter. I want something where it is affordable, where I am more settled and I don't have to go to a homeless shelter. I never ever want to be homeless again. . . . On my own I made a lot of mistakes, and I can admit that. Single parent, two kids, and one on the way. It [homelessness] not only hurts me but my kids, who are another generation. If I can't get to the point of stability, where can they have stability? You'll have three more kids growing up with the same troubles. Homeless women, we did put ourselves in this predicament for whatever reason, and now that I'm here and I need help, I need more. I'm trying, but I need more."*

David: *"I've been here for 2 months and I abide by every rule. I did everything so my kids and I can get a roof over our heads and start all over. But I'm at the point that it's like, I can't, I don't know what it is but I need help. . . . If I were single, I would not ask for help. I would say, 'Give it [the apartment] to somebody with children who needs help because it's getting cold.' But I have two children and moved 500 miles to give them a better education and life. . . . I have proven myself as a parent; check my record. I need help, I need help bad. I will do whatever it takes to get me and my children, my two sons, a roof over our heads. . . . I am telling you from the heart. I need to get an apartment. I need to get my kids a home, a second chance. The family needs to stay together. We need a roof over our heads to continue as a family."*

In the end, a few more families would be fortunate enough to be assigned public housing units in a reasonably safe area, but others would, contrary to their wishes, land in the same low-income, dangerous neighborhoods. Parents like Cathy and David, however, who have been languishing in the shelter for months without seeing any results from their house-finding efforts, apparently need more concerted assistance to bring forth a tangible result before their time at the shelter is up. Otherwise, they are at risk of being discharged from the shelter without a place to go or of being tossed from one shelter to another.

BARRIERS TO FINDING DECENT HOUSING

We expected that the parents' responses to our query about their perception or experience of barriers to finding decent housing would include long waiting lists for public housing and Section 8 vouchers, dangers posed by drugs, the low quality of housing and life due to urban decline, their low economic status, the high rents and their lack of enough money to make security deposits, and the problems caused by slumlords, because these were the factors that had driven them into homelessness. In addition, parents pointed out the hassles imposed by an inefficient and unsympathetic housing bureaucracy, the lack of transportation, the number of children, their eviction history, and the racial discrimination as significant barriers that they had encountered while searching for housing. Some also pointed out that their own mental health problems and/or substance abuse histories/habits constituted significant barriers.

When asked to talk about barriers, parents were almost unanimous in showing their intense aversion to and fear of dangerous neighborhood conditions and their yearnings for a better environment for their children. However, it was obvious that most parents, without command of the resources they would need to change their lot, also shared the feeling of entrapment in the poor and dangerous inner-city neighborhoods.

In addition to the barriers that the parents reported, we found that "shelter fatigue" was a contributing factor that put some parents right back to the point from which they had come. That is, they wanted to get out of the shelter so badly that they would jump at any chance and any substandard housing, although they were fully aware that such haste and desperation would likely bring another disaster.

Dangerous Neighborhoods and Affordability

Without exception, parents showed their disapproval of the quality of life in inner-city neighborhoods and wanted to find housing away from those neighborhoods. Even those who had lived in inner-city neighborhoods most of their lives did not want to go back to them for reasons of drugs and drug-related violence and crime, which were the most frequently mentioned barriers to these families' finding decent housing (see Table 6.1). The second most frequently mentioned barrier was

TABLE 6.1 Barriers to Finding Decent Housing

(% of respondents)	
Safety of the neighborhood	38.8
Landlord/substandard housing	5.0
High rent/lack of affordability	31.3
Lack of transportation	12.5
Racism	5.0
Other discrimination (gender and age)	5.0
Number of children	3.8
Eviction history	3.8
Long waiting list for public/subsidized units	7.5
Bureaucracy/inefficiency of public housing authority/ Section 8 staff	10.0
Own substance abuse or mental illness	6.3

their economic situation, which made it impossible for them to afford the rent, especially in "good" areas. Although, as repeatedly echoed by many parents, rental rates in bad neighborhoods were high compared to public assistance or salaries, apartments in what were considered good neighborhoods were more expensive and were beyond their ability to pay. Many parents also said they had trouble coming up with the lump sum needed for the first month's rent and the security deposit. (Moreover, many parents did not have much furniture, having lost their possessions in the chaos of becoming homeless. Only a few parents knew about the furniture allowance that New York State provides its welfare recipients.) Despite their fear for their children's physical safety and concerns for their well-being in bad neighborhoods, these parents were well aware of their limited choices because of these geoeconomic barriers.

Heather: "*It's gangs, and they are shooting all the time and drugs. I'm kinda scared. . . . I don't want to go back to the same neighborhood. I want to let my kids see a better life than the ghetto; I want to show them there's a life outside the ghetto. But there's so much slum area, and that's the problem.*"

Lynn: "*I want to get Section 8, so I can get a better spot, you know, in the city, so that I don't have to go back to the same thing I have been continuously running from, the drug-infested areas. You have to be careful about the landlords, the neighborhoods. It's drug infested! It's about survival.*"

Jill: "*The neighborhoods. I look because of my teenager. I don't want an out-of-control situation. Most neighborhoods are really bad for children. He [her teenage son] gets pressured enough. Also, we have a lot of bad landlords. So many places are not up to the codes.*"

Chris: "*[The inner-city neighborhood] is not fit for kids! We want to stay in [a better neighborhood], but the rent is a lot more.*"

Virginia: "*In the areas that are acceptable, the rents are really high. . . . I don't have a large income and public assistance basically has their guidelines in what we can or cannot get. So that's the biggest problem in finding something that's going to fit within my budget in the area in which I hope to get in. I'd like any area that is, you know, where the city is still accessible for, like, doctors and that type of thing, but I don't want my kids living in a rough area where people have guns and knives. They should be able to go to school without being paranoid of going, and somewhere they can feel comfortable going outside and playing.*"

Sherry: "*I want my kids in a good area; I want my kids to be able to go outside and play, someplace safe, but then there's really not much of a chance.*"

Lisa: "*Crime and drugs in the city. There aren't many good neighborhoods nowadays. That's one reason I moved down South. The expense of funding a place that's affordable in a nice neighborhood. My fiancé and I would be making good money, but I don't want to be paying all that money for a place I don't own.*"

Georgia: "*Not enough money. I can afford some, but not in the neighborhood I want my kids in. I can't do the security deposit and the first month's rent.*"

Andrea: "*I have no problem finding them [apartments]; I find all kinds. My thing is being able to continuously afford them.*"

Slumlords

In conjunction with the deteriorating neighborhood conditions and lax or nonexistent enforcement of housing code violations in these neighborhoods, many parents mentioned that unscrupulous landlords who take advantage of the vulnerability of poor people, particularly those on welfare, pose another significant barrier. In reality, in a tight housing market, most landlords would naturally be wary of tenants who are on public assistance, because poor people pose a greater risk of not paying rent. Then there is outright discrimination against the poor. All things considered, it is perceived that the poor would make undesirable tenants. Bonnie described the difficulty of renting a decent apartment because of many landlords' unwillingness to be beholden to the DSS for the rent payment of their PA-receiving tenants: "*A lot of landlords don't want to sign landlord statements or rent agreement with downtown [DSS].*" Under the circumstances, those who willingly rent to poor families either take such a risk for totally altruistic and humanitarian reasons or have little to lose in the first place. For the latter, who are largely absentee owner-landlords, the location and the physical condition of their property give them only two choices—either abandoning the property and letting it rot or renting it out to the poor, who are the only available tenants desperate enough to take such substandard units in dangerous neighborhoods.

Needless to say, not all those who rent to the poor are as unscrupulous as some of the landlords our homeless families described earlier. But the latter group is certainly present, and they prey on the welfare checks of poor people by providing rental units that are uninhabitable.

Tammy, who described how her landlord had taken advantage of her, made a very cogent argument that policy makers need to listen to: "*What galls me is that I haven't been gone barely, and he [the landlord]*" *has got someone else living in there on social services and he's gonna do it again, he's gonna do it again, because he knows that he can get away with it. . . . I told [the director of the shelter] that they ought to start a list of landlords that just screw people that are on social services. There's a lot of slumlords out there. [The government] should . . . have some way of controlling what they do. There should be some way if a landlord has an apartment he had to let the government know he's ready to rent it—I mean, they know he owns it. I know it's more money for the government to spend, but in the end I don't think you'd see as many homeless people sitting out here. . . . I really believe, since everything is going computerized, to keep track of landlords who are like this. Every time someone gets illegally evicted, it should go into the computer who the landlord was. They do checks on tenants. Why not landlords?"*

Waiting Lists and Housing Bureaucracy

Because of their financial situation, most families expressed a strong preference for public housing or Section 8 subsidized housing. A few families were lucky enough to be given an apartment in a public housing project, but most of the public housing projects and Section 8 subsidized housing have waiting lists that run for years. With the increasing numbers of low-income and homeless families, the supply of public and subsidized housing units has been far short of the demand for them. Many families perceived these long waiting lists as posing a significant barrier to finding decent housing. Others indicated that the bureaucratic paperwork and the unresponsive staff of the local public housing authority and rental assistance center (which processes Section 8 vouchers) were barriers:

Erica: *"[The local public housing authority] sent me a letter saying I had a five- to seven-year wait. The rental assistance center says it'll take 12 to 15 weeks to see if I'm eligible. I'm like, 'What? I'm in a shelter. What more proof do you need?'"*

Tara: *"Section 8 told me that there is a 15-year waiting list, and I asked them if I had to wait 15 years even when I was homeless, and they said yes. So I guess we're supposed to be homeless for 15 years. . . . The system is set up so you can fail, because they don't want any more people added to the list."*

Sonia: *"I went to the rental assistance center today and they didn't answer the questions I had. I am so in the dark about all this. I need a voucher. I didn't get a voucher. I need help, and there's only one staff there who would help me and she's on vacation. The paperwork process, the red tape and the waiting list . . . "*

Sandy: *"I have been here for 2 months now. I went to all the places I had to go, [the public housing authority], [the rental assistance center], HAC [housing assistance center, a social service agency], and another place, the four places you're required to go. What happened is that [the public housing authority] sent me a letter on July 26 to my apartment and they got it back, so they just put it in my file and assumed that I was no longer interested. And I was waiting for them to call me, thinking I'm moving. I had gone and told them I was in the shelter and did the change of address. So, when I went there, I spoke to the lady and she pulled my file and, sure enough, they had my change of address, you see, on the 17th of July. So it was their fault. If [the public housing authority] would have done what they should have done and looked in my file, I may have had an apartment a month ago. And now I'm here and I'm starting to think they are gonna put me out of the shelter, because they made me sign a paper the other day saying that this is only temporary, you know. I took the letter to [the public housing authority] to show them how serious the situation is. I've been waiting."*

Roseanne, a 20-year-old mother of two who got an apartment in a public housing project in 3 weeks, described how it happened: *"I was out walking to the places they said I had to go to, to the programs I needed to get into. And it took me, I think, 3 weeks to get my apartment. Three weeks, that's because I kept on bothering them [the staff at the public housing authority]. Yeah, they tell me like, 'You're driving us crazy.' And I'm like, 'Well, sorry,' because you know some of these people, there was one lady here for 3 months and they were not helping her at all. Unless I wasn't real active in reminding them, they wouldn't have taken time about finding me an apartment. The thing is that you've got to breathe down people's necks sometimes so they know you're there, you're real, you're a person, and you need some shelter."*

Lack of Transportation

Of the 80 families we interviewed, only 3 owned a functioning car. Without a car, many families indicated, their home-finding efforts were severely hampered. Many also indicated that they did not have money for bus fare every time they wanted to look at an apartment. Without a car, the families were also restricted in terms of where they could live. Public transportation is not well developed in the two cities where we interviewed these families, and thus many areas are off limits to them. The house or apartment had to be on a public transportation route for them to be able to do such basic things as shop for groceries and take their children to a clinic. Tammy told us how she and her family used to do grocery shopping: "*We walked to grocery stores. My daughter has got one of these baby strollers, and we used to get three bags of groceries in there, and they'd be lugging a bag each too. That's tough. And Alissa [her 9-year-old] gets embarrassed real easy and she says, 'Mommy, people are looking at us.' And I say, 'I don't care. We gotta eat.'* " Jan also told us that she needed to find someplace "*on a bus line for grocery shopping and all.*"

In the case of Angela, whose 3-year-old has multiple health problems (anemia, ear problems, and nose problems), keeping clinic appointments has not been easy. When we asked her if her son saw a doctor regularly, she replied: "*No, I had a problem with transportation. They [the clinic] have medical transportation. I don't like their medical transportation, which is a van, because they come pick you up late, they take you late there. And certain times when I don't want to be there early, they come early. But it's all right, it's OK. You know what I'm saying? It's OK.*" She was trying to convey to us that, unreliable as the transportation was, it was still better than having none because she had no choice other than the van service. Soon afterward, we learned that the clinics and health maintenance organizations that served Medicaid recipients in the area had canceled their van services as part of budget cuts and were offering bus tokens instead.

The lack of transportation is a serious barrier to these families' achieving and maintaining stability in another very important aspect, namely, access to a job. As we described in chapter 3, Jacqueline and Tony, a young couple, became homeless because both of them lost their jobs when their car broke down. Debby, a 32-year-old mother of two, also told us how she lost her temporary job: "*I was working for this temporary service. They call me when they have work available. Then they called me and I had bus fare for the whole week, and I had gotten off the last shift and no bus came. I waited for more than an hour and a half and finally called the public transit office. They told me the bus service stopped some hours ago. I had to catch a cab with my bus fare. The next morning I called the agency to see if I could get an earlier shift, and they said, 'You just can't come back,' because, you see, every time they gave me the job, I had transportation problems.*"

Lack of transportation is a significant factor contributing to a vicious circle of joblessness, poverty, and homelessness by isolating poor people in inner-city areas where they are not likely to find jobs and decent housing.

Discrimination

Some African-American families did not hesitate to list racism as a barrier. Noreen said: "*Some places are still, you know, a little prejudiced, a little hostile. But I believe God will come through for me and my children.*" Michael said with emotion: "*Color! The color of our skin, being a man with a son, you know, a single parent.*" Margaret mentioned racial discrimination as a significant barrier, in addition to the lack of income, a security deposit, and transportation. A few white parents told us that they did not want to live in black neighborhoods. Danielle said: "*What you'd call it, 'prejudice'—I don't like black people and I don't like drugs. I won't live in a neighborhood that's full of drugs. I won't.*" Tara explained why she decided to find her house on her own, although she, as a domestic violence victim, was given a priority for public housing: "*I was going through [the public housing authority], but forget it. They're trying to split up minorities and mix all races together. And they'd put me in a place where I'll be killed—you know, where most of them, like 80%, are not my race. Just to make themselves look better, look equal. You know, it doesn't matter to me, really, but some people don't want to be mixed, and I think they're taking the choice away from people.*"

Aside from racial discrimination, Jennifer, who is white, said that she experienced discrimination because of her youthful appearance: "*I mean, I'm a lot older than I look, and landlords think I'm gonna destroy stuff, although when I'm home, I want to sleep, because I go to school full time and work full time and I don't have time.*" She also told us that she believed she was being discriminated against because she was a single parent. Lauren, a 23-year-old married mother of three, told us of barriers that she had encountered: "*My age and my husband's age. We look young. People say, 'Oh, here's these two who had kids so young. . . . ' We had kids young, but my husband has always been there for me.*"

Many parents mentioned that most landlords would not want to rent to a large family. Brenda said: "*Six kids and being on welfare, they turn up their nose. . . .* " Heather told us that most potential landlords backed down as quickly as possible as soon as she let them know that she had four boys, because they were afraid that the children might wreak havoc on their property.

Eviction History, Mental Health Problems, and Substance Abuse Problems

When parents looked for housing in the private rental market, their eviction history often scared off many potential landlords. Wilma told us: "*If you tell someone that [you were evicted], they won't rent out to you.*" A few parents also acknowledged that their own problems with substance abuse and/or mental illness were barriers. Annette, who was a substance abuser and domestic violence victim, acknowledged that without cleaning up her drug habit and "*getting [her] life together,*" she would not be able to live "*in [her] own home, working or going to school.*" Renee said: "*It's a fact that, with my mental problems, suicide attempts, and depression, I can't work and provide any income for my family.*"

Shelter Fatigue

Fred, who had had to let go of substandard housing in a neighborhood full of drug dealers, told us that he had been "*in a different homeless shelter and hurried up and found that apartment in a month and jumped in it too fast,*" without carefully checking the building and the neighborhood conditions. It was after he moved in that he found that the place was infested with roaches and filled with repugnant animal odors and that he, a recovering addict, had "*moved right dead into drugs.*" Fred now knew how not to repeat such a mistake. But we suspected some parents could end up just like Fred, because of what we termed "shelter fatigue."

Parents like Brenda, who had had difficulty finding decent housing, often were ready to give up and take whatever might come along. It was partly a compromise based on their experience of the tough reality and dim prospects for decent housing, and partly their longing to get out of the shelter. They had just become tired of shelter living. Brenda said: "*At this point I just want somewhere my children can get established, where they can be out of a shelter. They say there are bad neighborhoods, but it's what you make out of it. If you stay in your house, you can make your house a good house. I don't have to be the neighborhood. You don't live in the neighborhood, you live in a house.*" Cindy, who was quite angry and resentful toward shelter staff and hated shelter living, went out and found an apartment in a hurry: "*I am leaving Monday—[an inner-city neighborhood]. I am just moving there so I can get out of here and then when I get myself settled, I'll move somewhere better.*" As in the case of Fred, her hurry may have landed her in a place where she would find it difficult to get settled.

Summary and Policy and Program Recommendations

SUMMARY

With the exception of a few families who had led lower-middle-class, stable lives, most of the interviewees had been in precarious economic and housing situations before becoming homeless. Their lives appear to have been a constant struggle to make ends meet with meager public assistance benefits and/or earnings from minimum-wage jobs. They had lived in substandard rental apartments or houses, usually located in dangerous neighborhoods, and they were frequently victimized by unscrupulous landlords who refused to fix anything and who ripped them off. Some had witnessed their loved ones being consumed by addiction to illegal substances; others had become sliders in their life due to their own addiction problems. Parents were constantly worried about their children's safety in the drug-infested, violence-laden environments. Most of the time, interviewee parents said that the children were all they had and that they were afraid that the children would be hurt or lost to the streets. Many women and their children had been victims of crime and violence in the neighborhoods as well as victims of domestic violence (which often occurred when the husband or boyfriend was under the influence of illegal substances). In many cases, the victimization had been chronic and had become part of their life.

As shown in the preceding chapters, some parents had mental and behavioral problems that precipitated their homelessness. But poverty was a predisposing factor for almost all families' homelessness, because it produced vulnerability to homelessness. The lack of economic resources had limited their choices as to where and how they could live, regardless of their wishes and preferences. It was also a direct precipitating cause of homelessness in the case of families who had been evicted for nonpayment of rent as a result of unemployment, the reduction in welfare payment, or estrangement from a primary breadwinner, as well as those who had had to flee dangerous streets and substandard housing. Poverty also limited their choices as to where and how they would live in the future after they left the shelters. Without some drastic protective measures, they would almost certainly end up again in the same places from which they had come, facing the same risk factors of becoming homeless again.

Thus, the most striking common thread in the accounts of most interviewees, especially mothers with children, was the experience of being constantly victimized by forces beyond their control, for the simple reason of their poverty. Homelessness was just one, though probably the most severe and painful, consequence of poverty. Most of the time, these poor parents were shouldering the burden of their misery alone. Some were lucky to have very supportive relatives, mostly mothers and sisters. But most perceived their informal social support networks as being nonexistent or frayed, either because they had not had such networks to begin with or because they felt that their previous dependence and their inability to reciprocate had thinned their ties to the networks. In general, their informal support networks were composed of people who were as deprived as the homeless families themselves, and the extent and duration of social support they expected from these networks was extremely limited. Due to their inadequate education and the dearth of informal support/resources, the parents had not had and would not have opportunities to change their life situations, unless support was forthcoming from formal sources.

Unfortunately, formal support systems or safety net programs— welfare and low-income housing—have had only very limited protective effects. In fact, they were designed to have only very limited effects in order not to encourage dependency. The scope of urban cleanup and renewal for the benefit of the poor residents is totally inadequate. Support services such as addiction treatment and rehabilitation and domestic violence prevention reach only a tiny fraction of those who need them. Worst of all, despite the thin boundary dividing homeless from other impoverished families, homelessness-prevention programs lag far behind homelessness-management services, which are provided mostly in the form of emergency food and shelter.

Some families entered a shelter system with the hope of gaining a shortcut placement in affordable low-income housing—public housing projects or Section 8 units. In part, the "shelter savvy" of these families reflected an informed, conscious decision, but it was also the only alternative left for the parents who, for the sake of their children, could no longer tolerate deplorable building or dangerous neighborhood conditions. Thus, even though the families indicated that they had left their previous address voluntarily (i.e., had not been evicted), the boundary between "voluntary" and "involuntary" leaving appeared to be quite fuzzy.

Most homeless families came to a shelter because it was their only alternative when they had become literally homeless. For them, arrival at a shelter marked a moment when life had spiraled out of control and they had hit bottom. These families were grateful for the food and shelter, and there was a shared sense of relief once they were at the facility. Many reported favorably on the supportive services at the shelter that were geared to helping the families with finding housing. Notwithstanding their view that the shelter was a boon to their families, who had nowhere else to go, the parents said that the crowded and noisy environment, inadequate diet, strict rules, insufficient staff, and condescending staff attitude added to their sense of chaos, powerlessness, and guilt toward their children.

Parents' anguish over their children's safety, hunger, residential instability, emotional well-being, and education was the most frequently recurring theme in our study. According to parents, many children were having an extremely difficult time being homeless and living at a shelter. All children were hungry, because shelters did not provide enough food for children and adults alike. Younger children were confused and agitated, and older children were embarrassed and shamed by their situation. Some insensitive teachers and school staff intensified the children's sense of shame and embarrassment. Without knowing how to handle their despair, the children became either withdrawn or hyperactive. Homelessness was eating away at the physical and psychological health of parents and children alike. Parents often blamed themselves for putting their children in the situation.

Despite these families' intense wish for stability, the barriers they faced in finding decent housing were the same ones they had faced before they became homeless. That is, despite the families' preference for public or subsidized housing units because of their affordability, the waiting period was still too long for those who were homeless. Coming up with the first month's rent and the security deposit was a big problem, and the lack of transportation was also a major barrier. Because of the constant demand for low-income rental units, most landlords are not going to change their attitudes and fix up rental units to make them livable. The landlords know that there are plenty of poor families who are desperate for any kind of shelter. Almost nothing is being done to regulate substandard housing and unscrupulous landlords. The law has always been on the side of the haves: Poor families who have been illegally evicted have had no recourse other than turning to overloaded, underfunded legal aid services. Moreover, some parents said that discrimination against minorities, single-female-headed families with many children, and welfare recipients was a significant barrier to finding decent housing.

Given these barriers, it is not surprising that most of these homeless families would end up in the same neighborhoods from which they had been evicted or had fled to escape drug-related violence and crime. There they would again face landlords eager to take advantage of them and be dwarfed by the danger of gangs and drugs. Despite their desperate hope for stability, increasing numbers of families were likely to go through the revolving door into homelessness. Almost all parents were fully aware of their limited choices, and many were frustrated by the dim future that lay before them. Although many of them took it in stride and used every bit of their strength to put together all the resources they could muster, some were utterly despondent about their future.

IMPLICATIONS FOR SOCIAL POLICY AND SOCIAL SERVICE PROGRAMS

From these parents' experience of homelessness emerges the need for a three-pronged intervention in the problems of homelessness. First and foremost, we begin by looking at policies and programs that need to be implemented to provide adequate housing for the homeless and to prevent homelessness among those most at risk. Some families may also need supportive services to remain in their housing. Second, we propose measures that would make shelters more humane places for the families who slip through the cracks and end up in them. Shelter programs need to be designed to alleviate the parents' and children's physical and emotional suffering that accompany homelessness. Third, we recommend educational and social services for children from homeless and near-homeless families, so that the negative educational, developmental, health, and psychosocial effects of poverty and homelessness on children may be alleviated.

Provision of Adequate Housing and Prevention of Homelessness

As illustrated earlier, the primary cause of family homelessness is poverty and the lack of affordable housing units, not the personal pathology of family members. Some families, of course, have mental and behavioral problems that precipitate their homelessness. Thus, supportive services are needed for the homeless, but homelessness cannot be prevented or eliminated without enough housing for the poor. Homeless families need permanent housing, and they should be able to afford it. The provision of permanent housing and the families' ability to afford such housing are also directly related to the revitalization of central cities and improved economic opportunities for poor minorities in this society.

1. *Emergency rent-assistance program:* Although funds allocated by the Emergency Shelter Grants (ESG) program under the Stewart B. McKinney Act may be used to prevent homelessness by providing financial assistance to families facing eviction or termination of utility services, the extent of this service depends on local governments' decisions. The federal government needs to mandate a significant portion of the ESG funds to be used for emergency rent-assistance programs for families at risk of becoming homeless. Rental- or mortgage-assistance programs for those facing a temporary financial crisis have proven effective in preventing homelessness in Virginia (Johnson & Hambrick, 1993). Especially in locations where the failure rate of Section 8 vouchers/certificates is high, long- as well as short-term rental-assistance programs are needed to prevent displacement of families who experience financial difficulty and face possible eviction due to nonpayment of rent. It is much cheaper to provide rent assistance than to house a family in an emergency shelter.

For homeless families, the rent-assistance programs need to provide funds to pay past-due rent and to cover a security deposit and the first and last months' rent to assist the families' transition from homeless to domiciled status.

2. *Expansion of low-income housing subsidies:* Long waiting lists for Section 8 vouchers/certificates in most cities must be dealt with

to prevent homelessness and to place homeless families in permanent housing as soon as possible. This may be done with restoration of funding for Section 8 substantial rehabilitation and new-construction programs. The federal government must restore its financial sponsoring of physical redevelopment and rehabilitation, designating funds to flow to the areas most adversely affected by urban decline. Private and public partnership in building subsidized housing must be vigorously pursued. Increased funding for the Community Development Block Grant (CDBG) would also enable local governments to carry out urban rehabilitation projects in dilapidated areas more effectively.

3. *More efficient management of public housing projects:* Due to the concentration of poverty, many high-rise public housing projects in large metropolitan areas are characterized by austere living conditions and infested with drug-related violence and crime. Moreover, because of flagrant mismanagement by local housing authorities, some large cities have vacancy rates over 30%, and many others have vacancy rates over 20%, while waiting lists run to years (Hinds, 1993). As evidenced by efficiently run public housing projects, however, the negative living conditions and mismanagement are not inherent weaknesses of public housing programs. Well-planned and -managed public housing projects can provide the most stable low-income housing. Federal government needs to increase HUD funds for modernization and rehabilitation of public housing projects, and HUD must enforce more stringent adherence to regulations by local public housing authorities.

Condemned public housing projects are often destroyed or sold for conversion to commercial development or for gentrification of an area without proper relocation plans for residents. Construction of low-rise public housing projects scattered in mixed-income neighborhoods must follow the demolition of stand-alone high-rise projects in poor, isolated black neighborhoods.

4. *Enforcement of building-maintenance codes:* Municipal governments must adopt and enforce better property-maintenance codes and make landlords responsible for proper maintenance. Local governments also need to implement early warning systems to detect buildings in danger of becoming uninhabitable and initiate an appropriate response. For landlords trying to make an earnest effort to keep up their property, no- or low-interest loans need to be made available for that purpose. For absentee landlords who knowingly neglect the maintenance of their rental properties in low-income areas, legal actions need to be taken. Landlords who repeatedly violate building-maintenance codes must be fined the sum needed to finance

the proper maintenance by a third party designated by the munici-pality.

In an effort to preserve existing low-income housing, local govern-ments need to take over abandoned property, owned more often than not by landlords in arrears of property taxes, before disrepair causes blight. State and city housing-rehabilitation programs must be tar-geted to the upkeep of existing low- or moderate-income rental proper-ties with appropriate restrictions to prevent market upgrading (Schwartz, Bartelt, Ferlauto, Hoffman, & Listokin, 1992).

5. *Enactment of tenants' rights legislation:* Poor tenants must be protected from abuse and neglect by unscrupulous landlords. Poor tenants need recourse, other than just inadequately funded legal aid societies and heavily backlogged local court systems, for the prompt review and resolution of illegal evictions. Tenants should also be able to file a grievance against a landlord who is suspected of defrauding the tenants or whose actions are suspected of harming the tenants' welfare. Strongly worded protective legislation needs to be passed for these purposes, with an administrative/judicial agency established to enforce the legislation.

6. *Information and referral services:* As many parents indicated, information must be disseminated to the poor families describing various rental-assistance or other housing programs that would help families at risk of becoming homeless remain in their housing or find new housing. Currently, numerous information and referral services are scattered under the roofs of different social service agencies and HUD programs without much interprogram coordination. Moreover, poor families are not provided with necessary information. A coordi-nated, central information and referral system is needed to facilitate easy access by the families. The system would be responsible for providing outreach programs, for disseminating information, and for linking the families to appropriate services.

7. *The Stewart B. McKinney Homeless Assistance Act for permanent housing:* The current focus of the McKinney Act on emergency shel-ters, transitional housing, and temporary services for the homeless must be replaced with that on short- and long-term rental subsidy for permanent housing, rehabilitation of abandoned buildings/houses, and enforcement of building codes in rental units in poor neighbor-hoods. That is, funding under the act must be used to prevent home-lessness rather than to supply emergency housing and services for the homeless. With the new preventive focus, the funding could then be used to assist those at risk of becoming homeless, reducing the pain and suffering of many poor families and saving taxpayers' money.

8. *Grassroots organizations for permanent housing:* Grassroots organizations modeled after Habitat for Humanity must be used to increase
home ownership among poor tenants by mobilizing them to rehabili-
tate abandoned or foreclosed units and by providing them with technical and legal assistance for property acquisition. The McKinney Act
and HUD must subsidize such rehabilitation and homesteading programs.

9. *Creation of employment opportunities for inner-city residents:*
Given that nonpayment of rent due to welfare cuts or unemployment
was the most frequently mentioned reason for homelessness and that
lack of money was the most frequently mentioned barrier to finding
decent housing, an increase in income will certainly be the best prevention of and solution to homelessness. Increase in income is most
likely to come with employment. The creation of well-paid jobs and
the improvement of the employability of inner-city residents through
skills-upgrading programs must be top priorities of urban policy. If a
realistic hope of employment exists, people will be far more motivated
to seek education and training (Fainstein & Fainstein, 1995). Low-
wage workers who are not currently eligible for job-training programs
directed at the unemployed or welfare recipients must be given opportunities to upgrade their skills.

10. *Improvement of placeability:* The improvement of employability
must be accompanied by the improvement of placeability, which
refers to "the perceived attractiveness of an applicant to an employer"
(Wodarski, 1995, p. 3). The long-term unemployed or those who do
not have a substantial work history may need to brush up their job-
seeking and interviewing skills to be able to identify and link with job
openings and to increase an employer's willingness to hire them.
Once they land a job, they may need to improve work performance
skills and on-the-job social skills to increase their chances of keeping
the job. Social workers need to provide the homeless and those at risk
of becoming homeless with comprehensive employment preparation
and training in these job-related skills through a job club (see Wodarski, 1995).

11. *Education and teenage pregnancy prevention programs:* No
amount of employment training and job creation can help those who
lack basic education. Given the high proportion of homeless parents
without a high school diploma, education should be a priority. Federal
and/or state subsidies for public schools in poor districts must be
initiated to reduce dropout rates and to improve the quality of education in those schools. In conjunction with the educational investment,
the fact that over half of the parents interviewed in our study had

their first child when they were teenagers underscores the need for more aggressive adolescent pregnancy-prevention programs. Improved education and delayed parenthood would improve many young people's economic status and chances for self-sufficiency.

12. *Transportation and child care services:* As indicated by the parents, the lack of transportation severely restricts their opportunities for employment as well as their choices in housing. The availability and cost of transportation can indeed be decisive in an individual's ability to engage in an effective job search and to take a job that is suitable for him or her. Because many cities have inadequate, poorly funded, and fragmented public transportation systems, a significant number of potential workers from inner-city neighborhoods have been unable to avail themselves of jobs in the suburbs. Others have been forced to leave employment due to the cost and time involved in commuting. Without transportation, many homeless people have a difficult time finding housing and managing other aspects of their daily lives. A solution may be vouchers or transport coupons in cities with well-developed public transit systems. In other cities, if a major expansion of public transportation systems is too costly, a public-and-private-partnership venture such as Wisconsin's Job-Ride program, which has been transporting low-income Milwaukee residents to suburban jobs (Nelson, 1993), needs to be developed. Also, zoning and financial incentives can be offered to regional and urban developers who can then cluster or plan to integrate public transport corridors with their developmental models (see Lowe, 1995).

Especially for single mothers, the lack of child care is a major barrier to employment. Subsidized child care programs must be available for all those who need them. Parents who work in low-wage jobs often need child care services that offer extended and/or flexible hours, because work hours for many jobs stretch beyond the conventional nine-to-five schedule. Sick child care services are also needed for parents with young children, especially when the parents are struggling with new jobs. Frequent absences from work due to caring for a sick child may lead to low productivity and dismissal. Children from poor families and deteriorating urban areas also need preschool and after-school programs to stimulate their intellectual and developmental growth.

13. *Welfare benefits, earnings, and health care:* To assure the long-term economic independence of poor families currently receiving public assistance, parents must be allowed to keep a higher proportion of their earnings and maintain their health benefits for a longer period before the public assistance benefits are reduced or entirely

cut off. Under the Personal Responsibility and Work Opportunity Reconciliation Act of 1996 (which repealed the federal AFDC and replaced it with capped block grants to the states), each state has the freedom to design its own welfare and welfare-to-work programs. The federal government must ensure that all states have adequate welfare-to-work programs that will promote the long-term economic independence of poor families. Especially for welfare recipients who lack education, skills, and employment history, each state needs to make a concerted effort to improve the recipients' employability before the time limit for their welfare receipt is up. The imposition of a 5-year (or lower) lifetime limit on welfare benefits, without a simultaneous increase in employment opportunities and child care, would only worsen the financial hardship of these poor families (Zedlewski, Clark, Meier, & Watson, 1996).

Another point made by the majority of homeless families in our sample who had been previously involved with public social service systems (especially county departments of social services) was that the welfare bureaucracy was full of entrenched workers who were not sensitive to the needs of the poor. Public social service systems are often besieged by ever-increasing caseloads and dwindling resources, and the line staff are often left with little time, energy, and resources to help their welfare and/or homeless families in the most effective manner. Given these limitations, preventive intervention with poor families who are at risk of becoming homeless may be an elusive goal, but at least a good-faith effort to disseminate available information may go a long way.

14. *Alleviation of drug-related violence and crime:* Drug-related violence and crime in inner-city neighborhoods will not subside without economic revitalization, which would reintroduce legitimate economic activities into the areas. Thus, ridding low-income neighborhoods of drugs and drug-related violence and crime must go hand in hand with the revitalization of their economic bases. In addition, increased police patrols and increased accessibility to drug treatment and harm-reduction programs have been found to reduce drug-related violence and crime. Local law enforcement agencies may also collaborate with residents of low-income neighborhoods to establish grassroots neighborhood watch organizations to combat and alleviate drug-related violence.

15. *Racial residential desegregation:* Federal support is needed to increase the spatial mobility of minorities. To alleviate the residential segregation of poor blacks in central cities, racial discrimination by real estate agents, landlords, or prospective neighbors must be se-

verely prosecuted. In addition, programs are needed to aggressively relocate individual families in subsidized suburban housing units. To make this suburban transplant possible, however, public transportation must encompass suburban routes. As mentioned earlier, public housing units must be scattered in mixed-income neighborhoods in order to promote racial and class desegregation.

16. *Interventions against domestic violence and assistance for domestic violence victims:* As discussed by the parents, domestic violence tends to be a chronic problem that requires systemic and long-term interventions. To prevent the escalation of the problem, social service agencies should make anger management and control skills and nonviolent conflict resolution skills programs available for beginning offenders. Through various psychoeducational methods such as self-assessment, individual and group counseling, role playing and corrective feedback, videotaped demonstrations, written materials, and positive reinforcement, individuals and groups need to be trained to build appropriate communication, social, and problem-solving skills as alternatives to aggression. Because domestic violence is frequently accompanied by substance abuse, drug and alcohol treatment must be offered with educational and counseling programs. Efforts to prevent violence are much cheaper and more effective than dealing with its consequences.

Women in an abusive relationship need to be made aware of their legal rights and the available supportive services and resources. In conjunction with an awareness of their rights, these women need to be taught assertiveness skills to enable them to exercise their rights and to take the necessary action. The victims need to be connected to resources that would help them find stable housing, counseling for themselves and their children, and job-training programs that would ensure their economic independence. Given the cost of sheltering victims of domestic violence, legislation must be introduced to hold perpetrators responsible for their behavior, both financially and legally.

17. *Substance abuse services for homeless and precariously housed families:* Outreach, combined with in- and outpatient drug/alcohol rehabilitation services and with supportive housing arrangements, appears to be the best approach. Emergency shelters must not just turn down drug/alcohol users but accept them and require them to participate in in-house or outside rehabilitation programs. Homeless and other poor mothers often find it difficult to participate in drug or alcohol treatment programs because of a lack of child care. The provision of child care is essential to facilitate their participation and

to help them stay in treatment. The needs of those with co-occurring substance abuse and mental health disorders must be addressed.

18. *Mental health services for homeless and precariously housed families:* As in the case of substance abuse services, outreach, combined with agency-based in- and outpatient services, and permanent housing with supportive services must be coordinated to provide stable lives for the mentally ill in the community. A linkage between housing and mental health services is needed to prevent homelessness among the mentally ill and to enable the homeless mentally ill to move back to permanent housing in the community as soon as possible. With the rising tide of managed care, it is especially important that the poor mentally ill receive quality services.

Toward More Humane Shelters

As shown in the parents' account of their shelter lives, the shelter has indeed become a total institution, providing a procession of the poorest of poor families with bare-minimum necessities for a short period, only to send them back to the same life situations from which they came. Homeless families who enter temporary shelters may be given priority in public and subsidized housing, but priority for one poor family means a longer waiting period for another because low-income housing stocks are limited. Given the lack of long-term financial and housing assistance for the poor and the tight low-income housing market, the mere Band-Aid approach of temporary shelters and emergency relief measures creates a revolving door of homelessness and underclass life.

Emergency shelters certainly do not provide homeless families with what they are desperately seeking: the stability of having their own home. The irony of this approach is that it is exorbitantly expensive, draining resources from permanent housing. Nevertheless, we cannot deny that, in the absence of immediate rehousing programs for homeless families, temporary shelters protect homeless families with children from the dangers of the streets. Shelters also provide safe halfway houses for domestic violence victims who lack private resources to fend for themselves. If shelters are here to stay, however, a more humane shelter environment must be promoted to alleviate homeless families' pain and suffering and to better prepare them to return to independent living. Both parents and children can benefit from improved living conditions in shelters and increased social services that would help them deal with daily grievances and the agony of homelessness. Specifically:

1. Shelter rules can be made a little more flexible to preserve people's dignity and to promote continuity in parental roles; dehumanizing institutional effects of shelters may be alleviated if the parents are allowed to be involved in rule setting/improving. Because families are constantly coming in and leaving, it may be difficult logistically to reflect everybody's input. Given the diverse needs of homeless families, it would be difficult to reach a consensus among the parents. Nonetheless, at least the creation of an atmosphere in which parents feel that they are allowed to have some sense of control over the management of their own lives and those of their families would promote their emotional well-being.

2. Some shelter staff may need added professional training to be able to better understand and communicate with homeless parents and to provide basic counseling for children. They also need to make parents aware of the need for counseling for children. Some staff may also need help with examining their ambivalent attitude toward the homeless they serve. Especially in shelters where rules tend to be rigid, staff members need skills to implement the rules without appearing to be disrespectful of the shelter residents.

3. Considering the depth and extent of these parents' suffering, mental health services are desperately needed to help ease the frustration, pain, and/or depression among homeless parents and children. Our study shows that many parents who had been victims of violence also desperately needed counseling for their posttraumatic stress disorder (PTSD). Ideally, the staff at homeless shelters should be trained social workers who possess the knowledge base and clinical skills needed to manage the myriad emotional and mental health problems that homeless parents and children may present. Because of shoestring budgets and staff shortages, however, most shelters in reality are not able to provide even crisis intervention. Thus, such services may need to come from outside, but shelter staff should be able to detect the need for the services and make referrals to outside mental health services. At minimum, shelters should provide a link to a source where the families can receive needed services or referrals to such services. For example, shelters can provide a telephone reserved for parents to call a hot line staffed by trained volunteers who can provide crisis interventions as well as necessary referrals to other modes of counseling services.

4. Shelters may better serve the needs of homeless families if trained staff can do a comprehensive family-needs assessment, link the families to appropriate services, and advocate for and guide the families through the maze of housing and social service bureaucra-

cies. Shelters provide information, for example, on sources of low-income housing programs, but then parents are left alone to try to figure out the complicated application procedures and to fight the obstinate bureaucracies.

5.   Children's nutritional needs must be met, by at least allowing parents to use their WIC vouchers and food stamps to buy nutritious snacks and to bring them in if they feel that their children's nutritional needs are not being met with institutional meals. Parents should be allowed to get involved in making decisions about the kind and amount of food that may be stored in the refrigerator, the allowed cooking hours, and the cleaning schedule.

6.   A quiet environment or a separate room needs to be provided for school-age children to do homework. Provisions also need to be made to ensure that children get enough rest and sleep. Curfew may be regarded as another example of an institutional restriction of individual freedom, but it may have to be imposed to create a quiet environment for the sake of the children's sleeping hours.

7.   Although most shelters are short staffed, their sanitary conditions need to be improved to prevent the spread of communicable diseases. On-site laundry facilities would also help parents in their efforts to keep their children clean.

Educational, Health, and Social Services for Children Who Are Homeless or at Risk of Becoming Homeless

According to the parents' accounts of their children's problems, it is fair to say that the children are the family members most devastated by homelessness. They are the most innocent victims of poverty and the ravages of homelessness, a human tragedy that appears to deeply traumatize them and cause damage to their physical, mental, and educational development. Again, the prevention of homelessness is the best solution to the problem. For those who are homeless or have experienced homelessness, we must provide extensive interventions to develop and increase their resiliency. Homeless children truly need a variety of services that would mitigate the negative effects of extreme poverty and homelessness.

1.   Given the high prevalence of symptoms of depression and anxiety disorders among them, homeless (and other poor) children who need mental health evaluation must be connected to services and receive continuous monitoring and, if needed, treatment. Especially

for older children who appear to have an especially hard time with being homeless, individual as well as group counseling sessions must be available at the shelter to provide them opportunities to express themselves. Experienced volunteers may be utilized as group facilitators. Given the frequently short duration of shelter stay, shelter staff may, with permission from parents and children, also need to contact and inform school counselors or social workers to ensure that they follow up on children (see Wall, 1996). Poor school districts generally do not have psychologists or school social workers assigned to each school. Where this is the case, shelter or transitional housing staff may need to refer the children for necessary services outside the shelter; teachers and school nurses may also be encouraged to refer children to mental health agencies.

Special attention needs to be paid to children who have been victims of or witnesses to street or domestic violence. Children who have witnessed violence against their mothers may try to hide their feelings and problems from their "fragile" mothers in an effort to protect them from further anxiety. Thus, the children tend to carry a double burden. Long-term therapeutic intervention may be needed to deal with their PTSD. More importantly, these children should be protected from further exposure to violent incidents.

2. For children, mental health counseling needs to be supplemented by other programs and services that would help alleviate the deleterious effects of homelessness on their physical, psychosocial, and cognitive development. Some shelters provide summer camps, after-school gym, and other activities, but others do not. In the absence of shelter-based programs, community centers, churches, and social service agencies can be the loci of recreational, educational, and social programs (with supplies of nutritious snacks) for these children. Experienced volunteers may be utilized as group leaders and program facilitators.

3. In addition to hunger, malnutrition, and communicable diseases, many preexisting and chronic physical health and developmental delay problems requiring medical attention plagued the children in the shelters we surveyed. Interestingly, many of the parents that we interviewed indicated that they had easier access to preventive care and health care in general when they became homeless, either because the shelter staff linked them to clinics or because one shelter had an in-house clinic staffed with volunteer nurses. When they leave a shelter, access to health care services may again be limited. These children need sustained medical attention, due to the nature of their health problems, such as anemia, asthma, and lead

poisoning, that are the products of poverty. Children with developmental delays, such as mental retardation, speech and various eye, nose, and throat problems, and attention deficit and hyperactivity disorders, may need long-term interventions to help them function fully. Continued Medicaid coverage and transportation to health care providers would greatly improve these families' access to health care services.

4. The many bureaucratic barriers (such as residency requirements and mishandling of school records) must be broken down since they prevent homeless and low-income children who move frequently from attending school daily. Remedial educational programs and recreational or social programs (with supplies of nutritious snacks) outside school hours must be open to these needy children. Improvement of transportation services for them is important, as are school breakfast and lunch programs. Although schools cannot correct the damage done by poverty and unstable housing, they can be a sanctuary for many children by providing continuity in at least one important aspect of their lives.

5. (Classmates, teachers, and school staff need to be informed and educated about the special needs of homeless children.) School social workers and counselors may need to develop a sensitivity-training program to encourage students to be more understanding, tolerant, and respectful of persons with diverse economic and personal backgrounds. In-service training sessions for teachers and school staff may also be needed to increase their awareness of and sensitivity to the specific academic and emotional needs of homeless children and to discuss appropriate interventions to promote these children's academic achievement and personal growth. Homeless children should feel welcome at school, and more sensitive school personnel will go a long way to ease their pain.

6. For the best results, an interprofessional case management system for homeless and precariously housed school-age children needs to be established. The case management team can be composed of a case manager/social worker stationed at a designated social service agency, school counselor (or visiting counselor in schools that do not have their own counselor on staff), school nurse, shelter staff, and volunteers who would provide tutoring, group activities, and/ or transportation. The case manager would identify homeless and precariously housed children, facilitate case management team meetings to establish and coordinate a system of needs assessment, service planning, delivery of services such as referrals to health clinics and counseling, and to monitor the effectiveness of services. The case

management team would also advocate and make arrangements for specific services that are necessary for children's academic progress.

EPILOGUE

Homelessness will continue to haunt increasing numbers of poor families unless we understand the relationship between housing and the changing structure of the urban economy. Low-income families face the double impacts of declining real income and increasing housing costs. As labor markets produce increasing wage and income disparities between the rich and the poor, and as housing markets drive up rent and swallow up low-cost rental units, the poor will continue to wrestle with a crisis of housing affordability.

Under these economic circumstances, no amount of effort geared to providing mental health and substance abuse services alone is likely to prevent homelessness among poor families and individuals. We have to tackle the root causes of homelessness. The revitalization of central cities, improved education and job training of poor residents, and the rehabilitation and construction of low-income housing may sound like unrealistic measures in the current political and fiscal climate, but these projects can be largely self-financing and even profitable, if prudent planning and coordination of resources among federal, state, and local governments and with the private sector are adopted. When successfully implemented, urban revitalization that includes housing construction/rehabilitation is a revenue-generating venture for obvious reasons: Jobs will be created and tax bases will be expanded. What we lack is not money but political will. All levels of our governments have been saturated with neoconservatism, which pits the rich against the poor.

The reality faced by many poor families is bleak. It is simple for lawmakers, politicians, and a majority of voters, who enjoy life far away from crime- and drug-infested neighborhoods, in which every other house on the block is either boarded up or burned out, to ignore the daily struggles that extremely poor families undergo. There is a chilling attitude across the country that equates social policy and programs aimed at improving the opportunities in and quality of life for poor families as "handouts" that would perpetuate their dependency and personal flaws. Compassion has been replaced by indignation.

We hope that this book serves as a wake-up call for renewed compassion for homeless parents and children. After two decades of inaction, now is the time to do something about the root causes of homelessness, so that the poor can share the fruits of a strong economy and enjoy

housing stability. We have to remember the pain and suffering of homeless families and their cry for help.

REFERENCES

Fainstein, S. S., & Fainstein, N. (1995). A proposal for urban policy in the 1990s.
    Urban Affairs Review, 30(5), 630–634.
Hinds, M. D. (1993, June 9). With help of federal rescue effort Philadelphia
    Housing Agency falters. *New York Times,* p. A14.
Johnson, G. T., & Hambrick, R. S. (1993). Preventing homelessness: Virginia's
    homeless intervention program. *Journal of Urban Affairs, 15*(6), 473–489.
Lowe, M. (1995). Out of the car, into the future. In R. L. Kemp (Ed.), *America's
    cities: Problems and prospects* (pp. 51–58). Brookfield, VT: Ashgate.
Nelson, T. M. (1993). Wisconsin picks up the tab. *Planning, 59*(12), 18–19.
Schwartz, D. C., Bartelt, D. W., Ferlauto, R., Hoffman, D. N., & Listokin, D. (1992).
    A new urban housing policy for the 1990s. *Journal of Urban Affairs, 14*(3/
    4), 239–262.
Wall, J. C. (1996, July). Homeless children and their families: Delivery of educa-
    tional and social services through school systems. *Social Work in Education,
    18*(3), 135–144.
Wodarski, J. S. (1995). Employment interventions with adolescents. *Directions
    in Child and Adolescent Therapy, 2*(4), 3–15.
Zedlewski, S., Clark, S., Meier, E., & Watson, K. (1996). *Potential effects of Congres-
    sional welfare legislation on family income.* Washington, DC: Urban Institute.

Index

Page numbers followed by t indicate table.

Schmutt